7/2039939.

UNDER AUNTIE'S SKIRTS

UNDER AUNTIE'S SKIRTS

The Life and Times of a BBC Sports Producer

Alec Weeks

Book Guild Publishing
Sussex, England

First published in Great Britain in 2006 by
The Book Guild Ltd
25 High Street
Lewes, East Sussex
BN7 2LU

Typesetting in Times by
Keyboard Services, Luton, Bedfordshire

Printed in Great Britain by
CPI Bath

A catalogue record for this book is available from the
British Library

ISBN 1 85776 962 7

*This book would not have been
written without the encouragement
and guidance of
Gloria Bristow,
who earns my grateful thanks*

Contents

Foreword by David Coleman

Television sports fans may not know the face but they should know the name. For over three decades it was on the closing titles following every major sporting event or programme the BBC televised. 'Produced by Alec Weeks' was a guarantee of a job well done. Nine Summer and Winter Olympic Games, fifteen FA Cup Finals, six European and World Athletics Championships, eight World Cup football tournaments and twice as many European finals, four Commonwealth Games, several London Marathons and dozens of *Sportsview*, *Grandstand* and *Match of the Day* programmes.

Many people would find 'Big Al' hardly their idea of a top BBC producer and executive. Within 30 seconds of meeting someone he is quite likely to be calling him 'cocker'. Indeed, an astonished Chairman of the BBC Board of Governors made the mistake of invading his outside-broadcast production scanner at Wembley during a match and was told, 'Keep the noise down, cocker, or you're in the car park.'

Alec started at the BBC as an office-cum-tea boy 65 years ago, during the war. He retired handling budgets of millions at Olympic celebrations, World Cups and Commonwealth Games – and he was never overspent. Television organisations, commentators and producers throughout the world regard him with affection and respect.

Of the current sophisticated system of BBC appointments he says, 'I'd be lucky to get an interview.' Yet the BBC can rarely have had more value from one of its servants. Effective, loyal, prolific and dedicated, no one has worked for the BBC with more pride. A 'nose in the air' young trainee once asked him how he came to get a top production job without a degree. The reply was typical:

ix

'You don't need a ... degree to tell someone where to point a camera.' Alec has a genuine and personal knowledge of sport, a clear technical understanding of what is required and the ability to transmit that to a large team of cameramen, engineers and commentators. He never left anyone in doubt as to what he wanted and expected. The language could be colourful but he learned the business in a tough school populated by television men of the calibre of Paul Fox, Bryan Cowgill, Peter Dimmock and Ronnie Noble. He watched and listened and when the opportunity came worked harder at his craft than anyone else. He loved the job and cared, too, for the dignity and traditions of the great events he was covering. Not for him the semi-artistic gadgetry that many producers, especially overseas, get between the viewer and the occasion. 'Let's get the basics right and we'll worry about the ... later.'

He always recognised outside broadcasts as very much a team effort. He welded his Cup Final crew together weeks before Wembley and when the moment came his voice would rasp through the commentary headphones, 'OK, cocker. Let's enjoy it.' The cameramen would all get the same treatment. The men on the balcony, veterans of the OB world, with their big zoom lenses trained on the playing area, would smile and lean round to the commentary box with a thumbs up. Alec was sure to get his team effort and there would be a few stories in the bar afterwards about the never-ending stream of direction, praise, criticism and invective that poured through the cans during the match. No one doubted he would (and had) got it right, and he thoroughly deserved the special award won for the coverage of the Final in '76.

His craggy face, rearranged in many a boxing ring, became a familiar and welcome feature of the international television scene.

Over the years we have shared a few bottles round the world and a lot of fun, and filled quite a number of television hours. He remains, as always, a loyal friend and good companion, and a trusted colleague. Nevertheless, he will not let me have a preview of what he has written. I only know his recollections will be as straightforward and honest as the man himself.

David Coleman

Introduction

I joined the BBC in the far distant days of 1941 and was with 'Auntie' for 46 years, 39 of which were spent in sports production. During that time the BBC was, without doubt the greatest broadcasting organisation in the world. Anyone who has travelled abroad and seen and heard other broadcasting networks will doubtless concur with such certitude. Throughout my time with the 'Beeb' I enjoyed the good fortune of working under some of the outstanding 'giants' of broadcasting, former Director Generals such as William Haley, Ian Jacob, Sir Hugh Carleton Green, and Charles Curran through to Alasdair Milne. In television I worked under inspired controllers like Paul Fox, David Attenborough, Huw Wheldon and Bill Cotton. All these men shared a basic understanding of what broadcasting was about; their aims were always directed towards one thing, the making of superb programmes. They knew their stuff from the bottom up; further, they always knew what was being transmitted, how and when.

1941, getting on for 65 years ago. That's a hell of a time to start delving into the memory bank. Back to the sound of sirens, bombing, ack-ack guns, back to the meagre food rationing but also the good sounds of the Home Service and Forces Light Programme carrying the mellow sounds of the 'big-bands', Tommy Handley and his *ITMA* gang, the deep bass voice of JB Priestley or Forces Favourite Vera Lynn. You got all of these for your annual licence. Ten and sixpence or 52 pence in today's money. And it was in 1941 that 'Dear Auntie', the Beeb, started all broadcasts on the European Service with the 'V' sign – the opening bars of Beethoven's Fifth Symphony. They were pioneering the air waves. Which is what I felt I was on many occasions during those 46 years – a pioneer.

1

Broadcasting equipment in 1941, though just about mobile, was heavy and cumbersome. Twenty years later so also were the television cameras, but it was in the 1960s that the speed of technical development in radio and TV was, at times, frightening. Extempore. One would often go out to televise a major sporting event with a piece of equipment which no one had used before or knew of its potential. Now that was pioneering.

I worked on the televising of sport for nearly 30 years, first in Manchester, producing shows in the studio, or on outside broadcast cameras. Back to London to produce/direct the studio side of *Grandstand* and *Sportsview*. But I finally got myself a transfer to the real world – outside broadcasts, producing and directing sporting events full time. Out of all the various aspects of sport I had been involved in in the broadcasting world, this was what I felt I had been put on this earth to do: OBs.

Today one produces or directs a sporting event. In my day one did both. Produced and directed. Organised the transmission, camera positions, the equipment required, the financial side, right down to the paper-clips, and then, the challenging part – the directing of the actual cameras to cover the event, be it soccer, boxing, athletics, racing or rowing. The opportunity to transpose the event onto the screen in the homes. Be it a world-shattering sporting match watched by thousands or a badly attended battle on a quagmire of a pitch. This challenge never left me. Put the viewer in the best seat in the grandstand and keep them glued there.

I have been fortunate to have met and worked with so many great people in the broadcasting world. Along the way I bumped into the occasional 'objectionable': I've just shrugged my shoulders and mentally filed them away under 'experience'. They exist in all walks of life.

Mine has been a fantastic life and I've worked with some great colleagues who have often shared many of the anecdotes that follow.

Interesting, yes. Historic, who knows?

I just hope that those in Sports Department today will experience that same frisson of excitement which I was so fortunate to live through from the 1940s to the 1980s.

Alec Weeks,
March 2006

2

Chapter One

Sound Bites – Wartime

1941. Bombed out of my Watford school. Father, an electrician, working out in the country at a very hush-hush secret establishment at Aldenham, got me a job as an office junior. It was the BBC's wartime HQ for Overseas Broadcasting – Aldenham House. I was coming up to 15. The salary was 10 shillings (50p) plus 2 shillings (10p) clothing allowance per week. I had to wear a dark suit, white shirt with stiff white collar and a black or dark tie, dark socks and black shoes. I cycled seven miles there, and when I got there I delivered post to the offices and filled inkwells. Then I cycled seven miles back home.

Two years on, the following internal advert on the notice board caught my eye:

Junior Programme Engineer
Based at Broadcasting House, London. Minimum age 16 years. Salary between £2 10s 6d and £3 14s 6d per week. Irregular hours of work. To assist the Programme Engineer in the Studio, microphone production of drama, features, children's programmes, news, etc. Essential qualifications: to be well educated, smart appearance, a clear diction, thorough knowledge of the technical method of radio production, including identification and knowledge of most musical instruments.

Not having any of these qualifications, I applied. The heavy bombing over the country had eased considerably. We still got raids, but not in a blanket formation over most of the country, and certainly not from dawn to dusk or dusk to dawn. Daily, light, quick raids over the cities now existed, as well as the hit-and-run type of raids

3

with the night bombers, such as the Heinkels, coming in low and fast within minutes of the sirens sounding. Bombs would be dropped, ack-ack guns would fire, and minutes later the all-clear would sound.

I was told to report to Broadcasting House, London, at 11 o'clock on 1st October and to see a Dr Alexander, BBC Head of Operations, in Room 812. I caught the tube from Watford to Oxford Circus. I walked up Oxford Street like a star-struck kid, which I was, towards this famous, formidable-looking, historic building, dressed then in its khaki camouflage.

I had been issued with a special permit that allowed me to pass the Home Guard security. There were a few minutes to wait in the magnificent reception, and then instructions to take the lift to the 8th floor, to Dr Alexander's office.

All offices were, and still are, on the outside of Broadcasting House, with the studios in the inner core. Once in the secretary's outer office I was promptly ushered into Dr Alexander's office. A smart, neat businesslike room, with the large window looking toward the direction of Regents Park.

By now nerves had hit me fairly hard. I had done no swotting for this interview, not really knowing what was wanted and hoping that enthusiastic ambition would pull me through.

Dr Alexander, who designed and invented the lip-microphone, was also an authority on acoustics in broadcasting, was a very well-spoken, smartly dressed Scot; his business suit covered a slightly plumpish fortyish frame. After a formal shake of the hands, he quizzed me on my background, schooling (no hang-ups there), my BBC career (very short) and my music knowledge. I had passed five piano examinations and could read a simple score, but that was my total knowledge of the music world.

Dr Alexander rose from his desk, walked over to the record player and carefully lowered the needle onto a spinning disc. The sounds of piano and orchestra thundered out. After a minute: 'Do you know the title and composer of that?' I shook my head. 'The orchestra or soloist, the pianist?' I shook my head. 'This...' he announced with a sound of disappointment in his voice, 'This is Cesar Franck's *Symphonic Variations*, played by the London Symphony Orchestra. Conductor Adrian Boult.'

I stared blankly at him; I could hardly say, 'How nice'.

'Now,' he continued, lifting the needle, 'I am going to play this

4

right the way through, and I want you to tell me, as it's being played, what instruments are playing. Identify each instrument when you hear it.' He turned to the record player. Just then the sirens sounded. Their meaningful wail making the hair bristle at the nape of my neck. Dr Alexander froze as he looked out of the window. Then after a few seconds he turned back to the turntable and lowered the needle. 'Piano,' I said within seconds of the record starting. Quite brilliant, as it was the only instrument playing at that time.

Just then a loud roar made the windows rattle. A plane flew over, low. Five seconds later the window rattled again as a dozen or so anti-aircraft guns opened up from Regents Park. Dr Alexander swung his chair round to the window, stared and swung back again. 'Strings,' I said.

He had a sort of fixed, half-smile on his face. 'Yes, but as there could be 22 different types of string instruments in a symphony orchestra, do you think you could be a little more specific and name the different types of strings?'

The recording was in full stride by now. 'Violins,' I ventured.

A double crump made the windows rattle. Dr Alexander jumped, then stood up. 'Yes, what else?' I could remember names, but goodness knows what they sounded like.

'Cello.'

'Good, good,' he said as he walked across the room to the door.

The ack-ack guns were now in full blast. He opened the door and went through to his secretary's office. 'I think I recognised a double bass,' I shouted. What with the noise outside and him being in the other office I thought I had better make myself heard. 'Guitar,' I ventured. Then, 'No, not a guitar.'

Pause for 30 seconds or so. 'Bassoon ... trombone ... trumpet ... xylophone ... big bass drum...' The names of any musical instrument that I knew I named. 'Bongo drums ... saxophone ... castanets...' Eventually Mr Cesar Franck's *Symphonic Variations* came to a finish.

The needle hissed and hissed to its rhythmic end. After about 30 seconds I got up and lifted the needle arm and stopped the machine. I returned to my chair. Silence from the outer office. I must have been worse than I thought. Not even a grunt reached my ears. I stared out of the window. Small white clouds appeared, each a second or two after the familiar crump of the anti-aircraft guns. The low distant drone of one plane provided a background

5

to the dull explosions. 'God,' I thought. 'What a test.' Beethoven himself would have had a job with that one. My thoughts dived between the test and what was going on outside. I was drawn, fascinated, to the aerial ballet going on in the sky. I felt at times as if I could reach out and touch the planes, they seemed so low. After 20 minutes or so I started to squirm. I wanted to spend a penny. I got up and went outside to the secretary's office. It was empty. I went back to my chair and sat for another five minutes. No one appeared, no secretary, no Dr Alexander. I looked at the cheap wristwatch that I had won in an amateur bout. It was just coming up to 12 noon. I had been in the office for nearly an hour. My heart went into my boots. I got up and left.

As I walked out of the reception into Regent Street the all-clear sounded. I knew I had blown the test, the interview. I could volunteer for the forces, boost up my age. Could I become a pro fighter? I could... And so on in this vein.

Two weeks later, back at Aldenham House, I received a letter: 'Thank you for attending the interview board for the vacancy of a Junior Programme Engineer... Therefore we are pleased to inform you ... based at Broadcasting House ... starting in November...'

Thank you, Mr Hitler.

A JPE did not have to know anything about engineering, thank God. I was trained, in two weeks, in the art of 'spot effects' and playing discs.

The spot effects storeroom appeared to me on first sight like a glorified junk store. Drums, motor horns, tin cans, bags of gravel and masses and masses of wood. At first sight junk, but those tin cans and bits of wood became as valuable to me as bars of gold. We were taught how to 'make noises'. By using the microphone correctly, spot effects could be an important and subtle background to a play, and yet, in light entertainment, effects were as loud as the artist, and in shows like *ITMA* (*It's That Man Again*) they became another voice, a voice known as 'cod effect'.

I was quite at home travelling and working in London. Many a day I would disappear into one of the numerous ex-news cinemas we, the BBC, had taken over, which had been converted into drama studios – for example, the Paris Cinema, Monseigneur and Grafton New Theatres – often reappearing in the streets late at night amidst a raging air raid;

Soldiers helping to clear up damage done by a bomb when it fell on a London subway, Bank tube station, January 1941,   © BBC Hulton Picture Library

7

bombs falling, ack-ack guns thundering, fire engines and tenders roaring towards the area where the sky appeared as an orange glow. Not many people were in the streets, the pubs did a roaring trade, but the shelters, and particularly the underground stations, were jam-packed. Three-tier bunks lined the walls of the platforms and at the foot of these Londoners also slept or sat on newspapers on the platform. Night after night the same people would sleep in these conditions, often occupying the same space, the same bunks, week in, week out. Sing-songs, to keep up their spirits, would echo round the tube station between 9.30 and 11; then it would quieten to a number of whispers and snores, interrupted every ten minutes or so by the whining and clanging of an arriving tube train. Here was safety. Up above was not just death but despair and ruin, even one's damaged and often destroyed home. But, as ever, the Londoners, the cockneys, drew close, helping anyone in need, revelling in the conditions of adversity.

It was amidst this style of life I began to learn the art of radio production.

The spot effects operator was another character, another voice, and he or she was treated as an equal. Many a time one of the cast would dash over and give a hand if, as was fairly often the case, three or four pairs of hands were needed. Tommy Handley was a natural charmer, never getting irate, always calm and always pleasant. The back-up cast was brilliant too, as Tommy might have a script, but ad-libbed all over the place, and excellent artists like Jack Train, Dorothy Summers and Horace Percival kept pace with him. *ITMA* was always a very professional, enjoyable, happy show to work on.

I must have presented a strange sight, a 16-year-old walking through the backstreets, late in the evening, making my way from the Grafton Theatre Studios, near Euston Square, down New Cavendish Street, towards Broadcasting House, a carrier bag in one hand containing a box of gravel, a battery-operated telephone set, a cabbage, and some string and elastic bands. In the other hand I would be dragging a three-foot gong. No one paid much attention to me. There was no one around. If the raid was a few miles away, over a different part of London, my footsteps would echo off the black, grimy walls of the silent houses.

I found the greatest asset of spot effects was that one had to use one's ingenuity and invent noises. Certainly, neither scriptwriters nor drama producers gave any help whatsoever; at the same time it gave one a completely free hand to experiment and to use one's own imagination.

Derek McCulloch's (Uncle Mac of *Children's Hour* fame) production of *Treasure Island* was a perfect example. One third of studio 3A would be given over solely to spot effects. Two or three of us would occupy this area, which looked like a cross between Brighton beach and the Woolwich Arsenal – swords, sabres, bayonets and dozens and dozens of 'slap-boards' – and if the battle was a big one we would ask for the help of any one of the cast, male or female, who were not speaking their lines at that time. I never really mastered the coconut shells. The horses' hooves. No matter what I did, my horses were always three-legged. If you are still in production and ever want a three-legged horse, I'm your man.

Once, as I was going down Welbeck Street to Portland Place, I walked through a nightmare of activity. A 'big one' had dropped some hours before; only the back wall of a three-storey house

1943. A grotesque sight near Broadcasting House.
© Hulton Picture Library

remained, the rubble stretching across the road. A bed hung grotesquely from the top of the remaining wall, and steam shot out from the centre of a huge pile of bricks. Curtains were hanging from the roof of a house a hundred yards away. A fire at the rear and base of the wall provided sufficient light for the dozens of rescue wardens and fire brigade staff to work by. Two rescue wardens passed me walking towards a clear part of the road, carrying what looked like a football between them. I walked on a few steps then froze. The grim reality of the whole scene hit me. What they were carrying was

9

The day-by-day life of the Londoner.

a human head. I had just turned 17. I remember many other things from that night, but also, as I scurried into Broadcasting House, I could feel the warmth of this huge, khaki-coloured building fold around me. I was safe and warm under Auntie's skirts.

Strange characters and geniuses ran broadcasting in that year of 1944. One was Lance Sieveking, the pioneer of radio drama; a huge man, head bent slightly to one side, a memento of a broken neck he picked up in the First World War Royal Flying Corps. I was working on his drama production of *The Thirty-Nine Steps*. Occasionally being allowed to work in the control room on 'grams' – playing effects records of actuality noises that could not be reproduced by using one's hands in the studio, such as cars driving up and away, planes, ships and trains.

We were rehearsing. Now Lance Sieveking plodded through rehearsals, stopping the entire session to get a particular part right before moving on to the next page. We came to a part of the script that took place on a railway-station platform. The climax was reached when an express train thundered through the station. Came the word 'cue' and I played the effect.

'Oh no, no, no, no, no, no, no, my boy, that will not do. I want a grey train. A grey train with pink spots,' Sieveking shouted from his seat by the studio window. Everything came to a standstill, all eyes turned towards me. 'You gave me a brown train.' I had been taught always to have spare effects discs in case the sound was not right, I certainly had plenty of discs of trains passing. My hands flew. Whatever this brown train was, he certainly did not like it.

Spare disc one: 'No, that's too blue. What else do you have?' Spare disc two: 'For God's sake, boy, that's green. You can smell it. Take five minutes' break, studio, this is going to take hours.' Spare disc three: 'No, that's black – pink and grey I asked for.' By this time he was towering over me. Spare disc four, my last. By now I could feel his breath shooting from his nose in his anger. I played it. 'I know this is wartime, but can't someone get the sound I want!' Sweat was trickling down the back of my neck. I picked up the original disc I had played five minutes earlier, but only I knew it was the original. 'Now, that's better,' he thundered. His lips cracked into what I suppose represented a smile. 'But it's all grey. Where are the pink spots?'

By now it was my wits against his. My cunning against his genius. My hands flew again. Lifted the disc off, put it in the rack with a dozen others, shuffled the other discs around and put back onto the turntable the same disc, that last one I had just taken off, the original one. My hand touched the turntable and my finger just moved the revolution catch to a slightly faster speed. Down came the needle onto the record. I slammed the volume arm to flat out. The control room reverberated as the train screamed through the station.

'That's it, that's it,' roared Sieveking, slapping me on the back with a blow that left me gasping. 'Back to page 12, everyone. Let's pick up where we left off.' I had played the very first disc, only slightly faster. If you ever want the sound of a grey train with pink spots, I'm your man.

It was about this time that I was told to pack a bag for a couple of overnights, and drove north with Harry Morris and 'Laddy' Ladbroke (the senior programme engineers), being briefed during the journey. Our 'studio' for the next two and a half days was the Corn Exchange, Bedford. My job was to be on the stage, with a band, and to move microphones around on instruction from Harry or 'Laddy'. A new type of microphone balancing was to be tried, a multi-mic technique; an idea imported from America, it entailed using one mic for the saxophones, one for the trumpets, one for the rhythm section and so on.

So I sat at the feet of Major Glenn Miller, and listened to the band of the AEF (the Allied Expeditionary Forces) playing the familiar hits of 'American Patrol', 'String of Pearls', 'Moonlight Serenade' and my favourite, his latest, 'Little Brown Jug'. I felt that, as an audience of one, they played and recorded 28 numbers especially for me. Glenn Miller's face was normally expressionless, grey eyes behind rimless spectacles, but his eyes glinted and his lips parted when a band member had played a particular cadenza with extra perfection. I was introduced to him over the loudspeaker talkback. 'So you're going to take care of us, Al,' he said, shaking my hand. 'Now you just sit down here, by my feet, and whilst we're playing don't you so much as move a muscle. Otherwise this band is so good they'll take your beat, and do you know what will happen?' I shook my thunderstruck head. 'We'll take your guts and string them on that guitar over there.'

And so for two and a half days I sat at his feet on this podium, hardly breathing, only getting up to move microphones between numbers.

He was always polite to me, even if sarcastically outspoken to his band. He was the boss, and everyone knew it and respected him for it. When the recording session was finished and the band was packing up he called me over to where he was standing, talking to Harry and 'Laddy'. 'Hope you haven't started smoking yet, young Al.' I shook my head. 'But I'm sure your Dad does. Give him these with my regards,' he said, giving me a carton of 200 Lucky Strike. He ruffled my hair and walked away.

Glenn Miller. At the end of the year, on 15th December 1944, the famous man went missing, presumed dead. But not his music.

It was in September 1944 that I was working on a programme that included, certainly in my opinion, one of the greatest broadcasts of our time.

Let me go back to just a few days earlier – 17th September 1944, to be exact. I was awakened at home in Watford before dawn by a rumbling, continual throbbing of engines above. The sirens had not sounded, yet there was all this air activity. By seven I was standing in our back garden looking up into the sky at a sight and noise I will never ever forget. In the dawn light the sky was black, with hundreds upon hundreds of gliders being towed by the ever-faithful C47s. The air throbbed with the vibration of their engines. There appeared to be only a few feet between the tail of a glider and the nose of the following towing plane. My eyes lingered for a few seconds on the khaki-camouflaged fuselage of a glider with its purple-winged horse of Pegasus painted a few feet from the nose. I tried to picture the scene inside of its 40 to 45 occupants sitting on the canvas bench seats in battle gear, dry-mouthed. The procession went on until eight. Then silence. I recall it was deathly quiet; even the birds had ceased to chirp. I had witnessed the flight into battle in Holland of the 1st British Airborne Division.

The Battle of Arnhem had begun.

From that evening onwards the radio gave us reports hour after hour. After a few days words like glorious, valiant, stubborn and courageous began to creep into the bulletins. It is sad but true to say those paratroopers were all those things and a lot more, but in short it was a battle we lost, together with thousands of men.

The BBC had sent two war correspondents with that airborne armada, Guy Byam and Stanley Maxted. Maxted was a Canadian, seconded to the BBC as a war correspondent since 1942.

It was 26th September, nine days after the beginning of the battle. I was working that evening on the Home Service *War Report*, always on air at 9.30 p.m., following the 9 o'clock news. The 45-minute programme had been on the air for 10 minutes when into the control room of Studio B5 (or was it S1?) strode a khaki-clad figure, who came to a halt just alongside me. He was recognised by one of the two editors, who promptly started to reshuffle the contents of the programme. The basic colour of his battle dress may have been khaki, but most of it was covered in mud and muck. His eyes were hollow and he hadn't shaved for days; thick, black stubble covered the lower part of his face, and dirt lay thickly under his fingernails as if he had been digging with them. He stank – a mixture of body odour and farmyard manure – and yet his wiry body didn't sag or bow. His dark, black eyes flashed everywhere.

He took a packet of cigarettes from his pocket – 'Sweet Caparoll' they were called – and started to write the odd word or two on the back.

After a few minutes he was ushered into the studio by the editor. Maxted took his seat opposite Frank Phillips, the announcer and linkman on that evening's programme. Only a table lamp lit the studio. Maxted waited for his cue. His iron-grey, close-cropped hair glistened in the light with perspiration. He stared at the packet of cigarettes in his hand, on which he had written six or seven words – his script. No other notes were necessary. Maxted had returned that evening from having spent nine days with our airborne troops in Arnhem. He took a deep breath and began.

'Kids no longer read books about mythical heroes – about knights in armour – because from Sunday, September 17th they'll have a story that should fire young Britons for generations. They were the last of the few.'

And so it went on for minute after minute. He painted a verbal picture of the squalor, the noise, the bloodshed, the bravery. Every word was clear, perfectly pronounced, strongly delivered, with dramatic pauses after certain parts of his description. In the control room there was utter silence instead of the usual noisy activity.

Late yesterday afternoon we were told that the remnants of the 1st Airborne Division were going to pull out that night. The enemy was making it impossible for the elements of the 2nd Army to relieve us. We were told to destroy all our equipment with the exception of what would go into one haversack. We were told to muffle our boots with bits of blanket and be ready to move off at a certain time. Perhaps I should remind you here that these were men of no ordinary calibre; they had spent nine days being mortared and shelled, machine-gunned and sniped from all around. When a tank or a self-propelled .88 gun broke through, two or three of them detached themselves and somehow or another put it out of business. For the last three days they had had no water, very little but small arms ammunition, and rations cut to one-sixth. Luckily, or unluckily, it rained and they caught the water in their caps and drank that. These last items were never mentioned – they were airborne, weren't they? They were tough and knew it. All right, water and rations didn't matter – give them some

Germans to kill and even one chance in ten and they'd get along somehow.

Stanley Maxted's broadcast to the people, never faltering, his deep, rich, Canadian voice was full of warm sincerity and, what all great broadcasters have, humility. He spoke for another six minutes, telling the millions of listeners of the great Battle of Arnhem, occasionally glancing down at his script – his packet of cigarettes.

> *Well, at two minutes past ten we clambered out of our slit trenches in an absolute din of bombardment – a great deal of it our own – and formed up in a single line. Our boots were wrapped in blankets so that no noise would be made. We held the tail of the coat of the man in front. We set off like a file of nebulous ghosts from our pock-marked and tree-strewn piece of ground. Obviously, since the enemy was all round us we had to go through him to get to the River Rhine.*

Stanley Maxted (left) and Guy Byam.

15

After about 200 yards of silent trekking we knew we were among the enemy. It was difficult not to throw yourself flat when machine-gun tracers skimmed your head or the scream of a shell or mortar-bomb sounded very close – but the orders were to 'keep going'. Anybody hit was to be picked up by the man behind him. Major Oliver had reconnoitred the route earlier on with a headquarters officer and had it memorised. The back of my neck was prickling for that whole interminable march. I couldn't see the man ahead of me – all I knew was that I had hold of a coat-tail and for the first time in my life was grateful for the downpour of rain that made a patter on the leaves of the trees and covered up any little noises we were making.

Once we halted because of a boy sitting on the ground with a bullet through his leg. We wanted to pick him up, but he whispered: 'Nark it – gimme another field dressing and I'll be all right, I can walk.' As we came out of the trees – we had been following carefully thought-out footpaths so far – I felt as naked as if I were in Piccadilly Circus in my pyjamas, because of the glow from fires across the river. The machine-gun and general bombardment had never let up.

I have worked on some famous broadcasts, been lucky to be present at many, many history-making ones, but that graphic account by Stanley Maxted that September evening in 1944 will, in my mind, remain as the greatest broadcast of all time. No autocue. No script. Just the ability to paint a verbal picture.

Everywhere I looked, or went, life opened up in front of me and introduced me to its amusing, tragic, hard character. As a JPE, I had by now, mid-1944, progressed to being allowed to handle simple single-microphone programmes – talks or religious programmes involving a single speaker, or a news broadcast. All these took place on the third floor of BH (Broadcasting House) – in Studio 3B, 3C or 3D.

The news programme only necessitated my being in the control room fifteen minutes before transmission, switching on the 'gear', speaking to the control room (then situated in the sub-basement) and, with ten minutes to go, having a voice check for a few seconds;

then sitting during transmission and moving a knob slightly from left to right, ensuring that the broadcaster 'peaked' correctly. The modulation of the broadcaster's voice moved a needle in the control room that ranged from zero to eight, and one had to ensure that it registered between two and six.

Got the picture, right. So, early one morning, about 6.35, I caught the lift to the third floor and to studio 3B to take care of the first national news bulletin of the day – the 7 o'clock news.

I had looked after a similar broadcast at 11 the previous night, had slept in a dormitory below the street level of Broadcasting House, and had been woken at 6 a.m. A quick cup of tea in the basement canteen then up to the third floor and to my first programme of the day. When one entered Studio 3B from the corridor one came straight into the control room, eight feet wide by five feet deep. It contained two chairs and, on a desk, control equipment, all facing a thick glass window. Often this window was curtained, but when the curtains were pulled back one looked straight into the small studio, containing a desk, over which hung the microphone, a chair and, against one wall, a small bed.

This is where the newsreader slept if he was the one to read the first bulletin of the day. No one was taking chances of the newsreader not getting to the studio on time. Often when one arrived they were up and awake, sitting at the news desk in their pyjamas and dressing gown. They nearly always dressed for the eight o'clock bulletin. So there we are.

I quietly switched on the control-room light and the few switches that produced the power to the microphone and, noticing the curtains were drawn, pulled open the two double soundproofed doors into the studio. The table light was on, but the newsreader, whose famous voice had announced world-shattering historic events to the people of Great Britain, was not at the news table, but in bed; or rather lying on the bed, or rather lying on top of someone else on the bed. All I could see of our 'famous voice' was the rising and lowering of his buttocks. The recipient was buried from sight, except for her legs, which were firmly locked around the waist of 'the Voice', relaxing and tightening in rhythm with his upward and downward thrust.

I stood frozen, looking at the scene for 10 to 15 seconds, my presence unnoticed. I drew back into the control room, letting the studio door quietly shut on the two lovers. I then acted brilliantly.

17

I sat down, completely and utterly shattered, and quite incapable of thinking correctly. I froze again, this time seated. After a few minutes the brain sluggishly functioned and again I acted in brilliant fashion. I turned the mic up. By now the rhythmic undulations had quickened and were accompanied by exhilarated grunts from 'the Voice', and squeals and heavy groans and sighs from the recipient. I recognised her from her sighs and groans: a beautiful, but very aloof, colleague of mine, a programme engineer, from a fairly famous family.

By now her sighs had reached an urging crescendo, and 'the Voice' was grunting louder and louder. It was amplified on my control-room loudspeaker and if anyone was listening for a test down in master control in the sub-basement...! His grunts, her sighs, were now in unison. Was this what they called the rhythm method? Well. I was 17, and the birds and bees didn't teach one everything.

I slammed the mic out. I looked at the clock: it was seven minutes to seven. I stood up and started banging and thumping around, whistling as if I had just arrived, hoping that all the noise I was making would get through the double doors to ears of the fornicators. A couple of minutes later I heard the outer studio door open. I ducked my head down and leant over the control equipment, as if repairing something, my back to the door. The skirts swept by me, just touching my legs. I waited a few seconds then walked into the studio.

'Good morning,' I said brightly. 'The Voice', sitting at the table, grunted a reply – a different sort of grunt this time! I left the studio and sat at the control panel. At two minutes to seven the editor arrived with the first page of the news, to be followed a minute later by the sub-editor with the remaining pages. The 30-second red warning light flashed above the studio window. I buzzed back, acknowledging that we were standing by. The sound of the Big Ben recording echoed from the loudspeaker: 'This is the Home Service of the BBC. Good morning, everyone. Here is the 7 o'clock news, read by...'

Three quarters of our department consisted of women. Youngsters like myself or elderly men made up the rest. As men were in short supply, even yearlings like me were in demand. One evening I was staying overnight at Broadcasting House, as I had an early start. This particular evening Mona suggested we go for a drink. She was a woman of 30, good at her job, with an attractive voluptuous figure. We had begun to work on shows together, so arm in arm we trotted round to The George in Portland Street.

The drink of those days was a 'black and tan', half a mild and half a dark ale. Mona could drink, and everything was in pint glasses, including my own. After three pints she was holding my hand. Four pints and, 'Why not stay at my flat tonight. It's just behind BH.'

Five pints and she was telling me that we could make wonderful music together. Six pints and she was telling me, in detail, the type of music we could be playing. That to me was like pushing a button, and within a few minutes we were rolling our way down Portland Street towards New Cavendish Street and her flat, stopping every so often for a kiss.

My head was muzzy from the drink, but my touch told me she was more than ready, and that certainly got the right reaction from me. I was rampant, to say the least.

We reached the New Cavendish Street house where she had a first-floor flat. She tore herself from my groping hands and inserted her front-door key. At that moment the quantity of black and tan I had drunk decided it wanted some air.

I was sick. All over the steps of her house. Mona took one look and quietly went inside the house and shut the door. My night of romancing was over. The following month I was called up. Mona and I never did get it together.

So I worked on *ITMA*, *Children's Hour*, *The News*, *War Report*, many, many drama programmes and many talk programmes, as I was based mainly at BH. One disc programme I regularly worked on, playing the discs, was *Sunrise*, from 5.30 in the morning until 8 a.m. It was always introduced by a member of the British Forces Broadcasting Network, which, incidentally, was based just around the corner from BH, in Hallam Mews. They worked on and introduced many programmes from within BH. One of those whom I got to know fairly well was Captain Ronnie Waldman, later to become the BBC's Head of Light Entertainment.

My call-up was getting closer and closer. I decided to be clever.

19

One day I asked Ronnie Waldman if he could get me into the Forces Broadcasting Unit. Just imagine, a home posting, and the opportunity to work at BH for the rest of the war.

So Ronnie obtained for me an excellent letter from the Commander-in-Chief of the BFB Network addressed to I/C Recruiting Officer, requesting my immediate transfer after basic training to the BFB Unit. A further letter from a BBC controller stating how brilliant and experienced I was, and I was then ready. I had to report on a Tuesday morning to a large mansion in St Albans, just nine miles north of my home town, Watford. There were about a hundred of us, and soon we were in one file, queuing to take our medical. I skated through that. Dressed, it was, 'Right, go upstairs and into the office, second door on the right, Room 2.'

Up the palatial stairs I trotted with my valuable letters in my pocket. I knocked on the huge, beautifully carved door: 'Enter,' came the voice from beyond. I was nervous. Being called up to serve in His Majesty's fighting services was a big step in any young

man's life. I patted my right pocket, in which lay the two letters that would guarantee my war and service career as a member of the British Forces Broadcasting Network, a branch of the Army. I wondered if they would make me a lieutenant at once. Those letters were highly complimentary.

I entered. The room was huge, in height as well as length and width. The walls were panelled in oak, and at the far end, at an equally huge desk, sat an officer – masses and masses of 'scrambled egg' decorated his grey-blue Air Force peaked cap. I hesitated, my hand still on the partially open door.

The author in 1946,

'I'm sorry,' I stammered.

'I've come to the wrong room.' 'No, you haven't, lad,' thundered back the voice, the magnificent chandeliers tinkling with the reverberation.

'Your name's Weeks, isn't it?'

'Yes,' I whispered, my heart pumping, my stomach beginning to turn. 'But it was the Army Office room I wanted. You see I've got,' patting my pocket, 'quite a lot of...'

'What are you blathering about?' the voice thundered. 'Today's Tuesday. You're in the Air Force.'

One thousand and ninety-five days later, I, together with the help of a few others, having rescued the country from the jaws of oppression, found myself working in the same place, Broadcasting House, doing the same job.

Chapter Two

Sound Bites – Postwar

About this time, 1948, I was assigned to sound-mix on a schools' programme called *Music and Movement*. A series of programmes to help five- to ten-year-olds appreciate dancing, with music from a piano. I sat through rehearsals; it was a fairly simple two-microphone programme, but I sat aghast, flabbergasted at the programme's subject. Unfortunately, the rather camp producer wouldn't listen to any words of advice from me, rebuking me with, 'May I remind you, I am the producer.' I rang a colleague of mine to get this programme recorded. At 11.40 a.m., we went on the air.

Good morning, children. Today we are going to play with our balls.

We are going to play a hiding and finding game with the music. Now this is what we do.

We pretend that you have got some balls, and I'm going to hide them.

They may be hidden high up by the ceiling (high piano tinkle) or they may be hidden low down on the floor (low piano thunder).

You don't know where I'm going to hide your balls, but the music will tell you.

Now first of all shut your eyes while I hide them – yes, shut your eyes.

Now open your eyes and dance lightly about looking everywhere for your balls. (Pretty 'dancing' music on piano).

And now the music is going to tell you where your balls are.

25

They may be high up, so you have to stretch and jump up for them, or they may be low down so that you have to bend down to pick them up off the floor.

Listen! (high tinkle on piano).

Well, were your balls high up, or low down?

They were high up, and I hope you all jumped up and got them. Now dance around, toss them in the air, and play with them (more pretty 'tossing balls in air' music).

Now I'm going to hide the balls again and I want the girls to look for them.

And so on for eighteen sound minutes. I had convulsions.

In 1948 the BBC were still recording on steel discs; quarter-inch tape was not used until 1950. Nevertheless, an enterprising recording engineer who was eventually to become a very senior person in television's outside-broadcast unit made copy after copy of this programme, and these were to be heard at the 'in' parties and gatherings for the next few years. I still have my steel disc in my record collection. Music and movement indeed.

As the khaki camouflage was scrubbed off the exterior of Broadcasting House, so the character of Auntie began to emerge from her wartime retreat. The scurrying home before the nightly sirens became a quick one at The George (Great Portland Street) for sport; the Horse and Groom (New Cavendish Place) for the feature department; the BBC Club (Chandos Street) for the news department. Cassandra may have had a laugh over the schools' 'Balls' programme, but he would have written a classic over the 'Steinway piano' incident.

Just behind Broadcasting House in All Souls Place, right opposite Egton House, was, and possibly still is, the main scenery door for the delivery or collection of large items of furniture or props. In those days the sound studios were always serviced by studio attendants known as 'brown-coats', as they always wore light-brown overall coats. It was their job to keep the studios clean and tidy, and to set the stage for small or large orchestra in the concert hall. This incidentally accommodated a Steinway grand piano, a rare and perfect piece for some of the best concert pianists in the world, and consequently a very valuable musical instrument in 1948. One sunny July lunchtime about 1 o'clock, a large van drove up to the stage doors and out trooped six brown-coats, who strode along the short corridor to the concert hall, and, with dust cloths and ropes, walked onto the stage. Another brown-coat had been there all morning preparing the stage for the London Symphony Orchestra the following day.

'Come for the Steinway, mate,' said the leader of our mobile squad.

'What d'you mean, come for it? Where's it going?'

'Down Aeolian Hall [HQ for BBC's Light Entertainment], wanted for Stanley Black at 2 o'clock.'

'Christ, can't anyone tell a soul a thing. This is the first time I've heard of this.'

'Always the same, mate. Didn't know anything ourselves till 12 o'clock.'

'Not your fault, chum. It's these … girls in the office. Gone to lunch, probably. S'pose they'll tell me 'bout it this afternoon. All their brains in their tits, and they're like walnuts, sod 'em. Well, there she is, be hell to pay when the tuner hears she's been moved. Tell yer what, you do the heavy and I'll navigate.'

So twenty minutes of 'back a bit', 'up a bit', 'down on your left a bit' echoed round the BBC's concert hall, down the corridor, and out into the sunlit street to the van painted the obligatory BBC green.

'Up your end, hold it.'

'We've got it. Slowly now. Lift.'

'Steady, steady. No. Hold it, hold. Down, down. That's it.'

'Good thing there were six of you. You'd never have made it with less,' said our concert-hall brown-coat.

The rear doors slammed on their valuable target. Into the cab the six of them climbed. A few farewells and off they went, turning right into Great Portland Street, the solitary concert-hall brown-coat waving them on their way. That was the last that was seen of the BBC's Steinway concert-hall piano. It was a gorgeous sunny day too.

Once upon a time there was a tubby little man who worked in the cashier department of the BBC. He was bald, apart from a fringe of hair around the side. He had joined the accounts department in the mid-30s and upon his call-up had served in the Army Pay

27

Corps, based at Aldershot throughout the war, attaining the rank of lance corporal, before returning to his mundane job at the BBC in 1945. By 1948, when he had just reached 40, he had achieved the position of cashier at the BBC's overseas-broadcasting building at 200 Oxford Street.

In 1948 it was only the very senior and highly paid employees of the corporation who were paid monthly. The rest of the staff collected their salaries in little brown square envelopes on a Friday. So on this particular Friday, as had been his habit since returning from the forces, the little cashier walked the 380 yards from 200 Oxford Street to the BBC cashier department at the foot of Portland Place, just across the road from Broadcasting House, reaching there exactly at 9.30 a.m., to collect the wages for the 350-odd members of 200 Oxford Street, to be ready for their insatiable demands by 10.30 a.m. It was a lovely sunny morning. Nevertheless, he still wore his bowler hat, and carried his umbrella in one hand and his large black lockable briefcase in the other. His efficient, expert hands swiftly transferred the numerous pay packets, totalling just over £22,000, from the large safe into his briefcase, under the watchful eye, of course, of one of the corporation's hallowed chief cashiers.

Our little cashier checked the pay-packet numbers and duly signed the receipt register. Then, after carefully locking his briefcase, he bid his colleagues 'Good morning', replaced his bowler, and together with his trusted umbrella caught the lift from the second to the ground floor and strolled briskly into the brilliant sunshine of Portland Place. He has never been seen since!

On occasions, I can visualise our little man sitting on a beach on some far distant Pacific island: a drink in one hand, a dusky maiden in the other, and with his briefcase at his feet, on his head, at a slightly jaunty angle, his black bowler hat. I think I saw him last year on one of the Caribbean islands.

Everything seemed to happen in 1948. It was in that year that a 'mad' Scotsman named Angus McKay finally convinced the powers-that-be to give him a 30-minute spot on what was then the Light Programme at 5 o'clock on a Saturday evening.

I was fortunate to be assigned that programme to 'look after' as a studio manager upon my return from the forces, which I did until about 1953. Angus McKay 'found' (he introduced) Eamon Andrews, Peter West and Max Robertson; he also revolutionised the presentation of sport, and set a pattern which still exists today. By his extensive use of post-office lines he was able to include reports on every major sporting event of that day – 30 seconds here, 30 seconds there. His *Sports Report*, which was quickly extended to one-hour duration, always had the last 20 to 25 minutes consisting of studio discussions between experts and journalists on some topical sporting subject of the day. There was the time in '49 when Fred Perry, Peter Wilson, Jim Manning and Joe Louis in New York were discussing some aspect of international sport, but throughout those first few minutes this loud and continuous banging noise could be heard.

'We have a faulty microphone cable,' I shouted to Angus.

As I was using 4 or 5 mics, I couldn't find out which one it was, but all the time there was this rhythmic knocking noise.

'Leave it to me,' shouted Angus and disappeared into the studio.

I hadn't a clue where he'd gone until I looked, whereupon I had, for the next few minutes, a ringside seat. Angus McKay was on his hands and knees, following all the different microphone cables *under* the discussion table until he found one that had somehow got right onto Peter Wilson's chair. Wilson was sitting on it. Angus traced the cable up Wilson's ankle, up his leg, along his thigh, and right under his bottom. Without any hesitation Angus put one hand under Wilson's groin, right under his testicles, and pushed up slightly. Up to that moment, Peter Wilson had been in full vocal flight. As this hand grasped and pushed under his testicles he rose slightly, his face going bright red, and his voice took on a much higher pitch, finishing the sentence with a strangling, gurgling croak that disappeared in a whisper. Under the table, Angus McKay took this opportunity to pull the cable free from any 'obstacles', and the knocking of the microphone cable stopped. Eamonn Andrews, with Wilson drying up quickly, called in another speaker and the discussion continued, minus by now a very red-faced Peter Wilson, who was visibly shaking with the emotion of the experience he had just gone through. It is not often that whilst one is broadcasting a hand commences to grasp one's testicles.

But, with Angus McKay, anything could happen.

* * *

29

Making radio programmes in one's spare time became the in-thing. I palled up with another workaholic named Harry Rogers, and we dived around all over the country recording programmes on this or that for *Children's Hour*, *Woman's Hour*, etc., often earning an extra fiver on top of our wages. Some people thought it was cheap labour; it was, but we were buying something not on the shelves or in the books – experience.

One programme got us into trouble, a programme on holiday campers, recorded at Butlin's Holiday Camp. We had been trusted with one of the six portable tape recorders the BBC had just purchased. We intended our programme to include a flavour from every part of the holiday camp: the canteen, swimming pool, funfair, music hall, concert hall, the bars and the gymnasium. Unfortunately, or fortunately, the day we were there the gym had an open boxing tournament.

'Go on, Alec, in you go. Let's show the listeners we're not cissies,' says Harry. 'I'll do a commentary, we'll get the audience reaction, it'll make a great recording.'

Now, Harry had a great way of talking people into saying 'yes'. Minutes later I heard a voice saying, 'OK, I'll have a go.' The voice was mine. About 1.30 we wandered over to the camp's gymnasium, which was slowly filling up, found a dressing room, and Harry, who had rustled up some kit – shorts, vest, tennis shoes that fitted – departed mumbling something about seeing officials. I started to change.

'I've seen your sparring partner,' he shouted as he burst in 10 minutes later, 'I just said we should all take it easy, put on an exhibition. You keep an eye on me, and when I give you the thumbs up you know I'm recording, so just move a bit faster. You know, show off. If I give you the thumbs down I've got trouble with the tape.' I was about to ask him how this 'exhibition' was going to finish when he dashed out again. Harry was enjoying his role of fight-manager-cum-radio-producer-cum-engineer. Yes, engineer. More about that later. After the endless nerve-racking wait, Harry suggested we make our way down to the ring. We were halfway there, and the result of the previous bout was just about to be announced, when I stopped.

'Look, Harry, another fight is about to start.' A heavyweight was climbing into the ring.

'That's not the next bout,' said Harry. 'That's your opponent.'

30

Once inside the ropes I realised this fellow weighed at least 14 stone (to my 11½ stone – I was a middleweight). He seemed to dwarf me. Indeed he did dwarf me.

'Put on an exhibition – enjoy it,' said Harry as the bell went. So I was on my toes, moving around, arms moving, flicking out my glove, hitting his arms and shoulders with my open glove. I went into a clinch every twenty seconds or so and looked over, or sometimes under, this fellow's shoulder to where Harry was sitting with the tape recorder on his knee. He glanced up, gave me the thumbs down and then returned to concentrating on the portable recorder.

All of a sudden I'm 'aware' of this swishing noise around my ears. I realise quickly this opponent of mine is trying to knock my head off. This gorilla obviously does not understand the words 'exhibition' or 'take it easy'. I move, back-pedal and clinch. With each clinch I look at Harry. Thumbs down. After a while the referee is warning me for holding, and, just on the bell, for not trying. As I move around the ring I realise this fellow means business, he wants to have an early bath and go back to his beer on the bar. I go to the corner and plonk myself on the stool. Harry is already there. 'We've got problems.' Here we go. I'm inside the ring, sweat running down my face. Harry's outside and *we've* got problems!

Now, a few years earlier Harry and I had been sent to the BBC's engineering school in Evesham. A complete waste of time, or so I thought. But not so, for Harry then proceeded, for 55 seconds, to give me a complete technical breakdown of the mechanical workings of the EMI portable tape recorder. Now when the Marquis of Queensbury devised the rules of boxing, one law for a short intermission between each round was brought in for the contestants to rest mind and body, not to receive a lecture on Ohm's Law.

Seconds out. 'Remember, we've got problem,' shouts Harry. The bell finds me in a very bemused and brainwashed state in the centre of the ring. The gorilla comes out like a man possessed. He's swinging blows like sledgehammers, gloves whistling past my chops like thunderbolts. I'm hoping it's a quick flash, but, no, he keeps going, determined to knock my head off. I clinch. Look at Harry. Thumbs down. Another referee's warning. I break, dance, clinch.

Thumbs up! It's all systems go. I take half a step back, slide my right foot forward, and bang over a smart hard left hook, slightly harder and faster than I had intended. That's it. Down he goes. He'll certainly have an early bath, old boy.

Back in the corner there's Harry again. 'Cutting that a bit fine. I only had five seconds of tape left.'

Unfortunately, the reaction was not one of 'Hail the conquering hero'. My final attack on my opponent had dislodged a couple of his teeth, which he had bitterly explained to a newspaper reporter from the *Evening Standard*, and which of course was in the evening editions by the time we got back to town.

I duly received a lecture from my superiors on how to treat the public. But my superior was not in the ring with a gorilla!

I found these years not only informative but educational. My interest in sport was generally known. I was loaned, as a programme assistant, to Outside Broadcasts department quite regularly, for holiday relief etc., I didn't mind. I knew I would be studying another aspect of production – commentating. We were normally a team of three, commentator, producer and engineer. This was increased by a further two or three for a major event. I was soon observing the right and wrong way to use the voice; how to raise one's voice above a baying crowd by using the stomach, not just the larynx, the voice then lasting longer. The use of 'light' and 'shade' to emphasize a point. When to speed up the commentary. When to use more volume. Rex Alston for example, had all these attributes, together with thorough preparation and writing-up of notes before arriving at the event. This was how he could articulate for hours on end on cricket, athletics, rugby and many other subjects. Raymond Glendenning could accelerate and increase his volume within two words, so also could Stewart Macpherson. Controlled breathing enabled all these, together with Max Robertson and Alan Clarke, to speak at some length, in long sentences, without pausing for breath. The right tones were also a great asset to the commentator; John Arlott, Peter West, and Raymond Baxter had these 'smooth' tones.

And as I sat alongside these commentators I was able to judge when and how tense they became prior to transmission; some became so 'detached' no one alongside them existed. But, in their own way, they were very professional and none more so than those two supreme broadcasters who lived up to the highest standards of all commentators. I speak of Wynford Vaughan-Thomas and Richard

Dimbleby, who besides having all the above qualities had wonderful voices and a great command of the Queen's English.

Some were still to become household names, none more so than Eamon Andrews whose move onto *Sports Report* was the start of a sensational broadcasting career. I noticed the way he had control over a discussion involving five or six experts, using his fingers to signal a move to another speaker, or the change to another subject, with each slight move of his hand sending a signal, a message, to the panel around him.

I spent many months working with these 'voices' and gradually they began to rely on me to be a second pair of eyes, to help them overcome a problem or a mistake.

This was the time I was able to absorb mentally the many aspects of the commentator's method of working. And I used this knowledge in future years. How are today's producers trained?

From 1955 until the end of '58 I had a great job in radio. I was in charge of sport on the BBC's GOS – General Overseas Service. A wonderful job. Come 1958 we had the Commonwealth Games at Cardiff. I took a team of three down to Cardiff, and, besides relaying commentary transmitted on the BBC's Light Programme, our main job was to obtain interviews with various overseas competitors. It didn't matter who these competitors were as long as they were competing in the Games. I and my team would go around the streets of the competitors' village, around their canteen, in the cinemas, anywhere, sticking our microphones under anyone's nose; if they were black, sepia, yellow, it didn't matter a damn: we just gathered the ad-hoc interviews.

But, in the event, whoever we interviewed for a minute or two (and they each always finished with a message back home 'with love to Mum!'), whoever they were, would, that day, that evening, go out on to the track, into the pool, ring, arena, and not only win a gold medal, but often would break a world record.

We would stop a tracksuited Kenyan in the street who, that evening, would win the steeplechase gold; or a skinny-looking competitor from India who, that afternoon, would win the flyweight wrestling title; or interrupt a beautiful blonde Australian Sheila over her breakfast who, that afternoon, would win the women's 400 yards freestyle swimming title.

This went on and on throughout the ten days of the Games. We just could not miss. Everyone we spoke to 'turned to gold'. To overseas listeners in Nairobi, Perth, Auckland, Bombay, etc., my team and I were famous!

When I returned to London my boss, Stuart Hood, said, 'If you are ever thinking of moving into television, Alec, do it now. Whilst your name is on everyone's lips. Don't wait until they are scratching their heads and saying, "Alec who?" Apply for a job in the regions and get experience.'

Back in our Chiswick flat, my wife Pamela and I sat down and made a list of the BBC regions we preferred, starting with Bristol, 'nice countryside'; second choice Belfast, 'nice people in Belfast'; third, Glasgow, 'oh, those Highlands'; and so forth until the tenth and last on the list, Manchester, 'it's always raining, and whoever chooses to live that far north of the Watford Gap? Injun territory!'

Chapter Three

A Dog, a Cat, a Horse and The King

In November 1958 I transferred to television ... in Manchester. I was a sports production assistant for that first year, but I was prepared to do any job provided I could learn something about my new trade.

A Dog

So for the first few months I just buried myself in every aspect of television I could find, from sweeping the studio floor to costume and set design, to vision mixing in drama. A former colleague in radio, one Johnny Ammonds, had found a couple of up-and-coming comedians and talked the head of programmes into a series of 30-minute northern-opt-out programmes – he had me as his floor manager for six of those programmes. I was not the only one learning about television; the two comedians were also doing the same thing. Morecambe and Wise learnt quickly. So it went on, with me directing a two-minute spot there or a five here. Then came my first outside-broadcast assignment: the TV Greyhound Final, White City Stadium, Manchester. I had two weeks to prepare. Having studied film after film of previous finals, I held a planning meeting at the track to position the four cameras, though it was the senior engineer who guided me into the best positions. The 15-minute item was an insert into the regular Wednesday night programme *Sportsview*. I had the list of the six finalists, three each from the two semi-finals two weeks earlier. I went through these with Harry Carpenter back at his hotel the evening before, this after having spent the best part of the day seeing the equipment in and liaising with the stadium officials. I left Harry about 10 p.m. satisfied that all was ready.

Just as I arrived at the stadium the following morning – transmission day – a phone call from the sports department in London informed me that the favourite had been withdrawn because of injury to its foot, to be replaced by one of the reserve dogs from the semi-finals. This particular dog had come fourth and was given no chance whatsoever in the Greyhound Final, which otherwise consisted of genuine classy runners. Our reserve was quoted on the betting by early evening at 18 to 1 – mighty high odds, even for a six-dog race.

The afternoon was spent rehearsing, sorting out camera shots, angles, etc. I had even arranged a couple of trial races, three mature (elderly) dogs per race. During these I was aware of some pretty heavy swearing. After the trials I enquired on talkback as to whether someone had had some technical problems during the races. 'Alec,' said my senior cameraman over talkback, 'if you had to pan these bloody heavy cameras at the speed these clapped-out dogs were travelling and pull focus at the same time, you would be swearing.'

During the next few hours I mentally went through every cut on the mixer bank, concentrating on nothing but the direction of the cameras. The dogs could all have been from Disneyland. *Sportsview* went on the air and after the headlines, etc., Peter Dimmock, the compère in London, announced, 'Let's start our programme with the big event in the greyhound-racing world, the TV Greyhound Trophy, and here to set the scene at Manchester is Harry Carpenter.' Away we went. My first OB. I was completely oblivious to any of Harry's commentary; he could have been describing the Royal Procession. I concentrated just on the pictures. The crowds, the gigantic forever-moving illuminated Tote board, the punters, the bookies, close-ups of the greyhounds' faces, even the scruffy brindle dog in trap six, the one with the white nose, the reserve at 18 to 1. It was all going well, the excitement was building up, and then the hare was running, filling the screen with its bobbly movement. A close-up of the traps, dogs' noses and yelping. Up. They're off!

The next 45 seconds flash by in a blur – 850 yards. Just for a second six dogs side by side charge into the first corner. Two tumble out at the first bend, forever doomed to fight out the fifth and sixth places. Down they flash into the back straight, by now nose to tail. The lead changes as they come into the next bend and burst past the finishing line for the first time. Now they are really moving, and so are my fingers over the mixer; even more so are the cameras, the voices controlling them swearing ninety to the dozen, cursing every hair on the dogs' backs. The front three are gradually separating themselves from the others. As they tear into the last bend each dog is forcing its muscles forward, up and under its stomach, each muscle standing out like the precision part of a rippling, flowing machine. As they explode into the finishing straight I see a flash of black and brindle, honey and white paws, even a small white nose, and as they reach for the illuminated finishing line white teeth are bared and snarling within their wired muzzles.

The roaring of the crowd reached a crescendo, practically a screaming, moaning roar, as that one nose seemed to project itself in front of the others. A photo finish. 'Give us a close-up of the winner, Manchester,' boomed the disembodied voice over the talkback loudspeaker from London. 'Then over the close-up, Harry, give us who you think is the winner.'

I asked for a close-up of the winner. Two or three kennel girls were fussing around the winner. They knew who had won, beside the dog itself, who, standing still for the first time since the off, was allowing himself to be bedecked in a purple-and-green jacket with the words embroidered in gold, 'TV GREYHOUND CHAMPION – 1958'. His lungs were still working overtime, and he still seemed to be gulping huge chunks of air into himself, his panting taking the form of patches of steam pouring from his mouth. The handlers had just finished and I cut to a full-length shot of the new champion, the proud four-legged winner filling the screen. He looked directly at our lens; he surely must have sensed my presence. He then lifted his leg and peed straight toward the camera. The jet came out of him at a pretty high velocity, all this in close-up over Harry's closing words recapping on the winner. Harry ignored the champion's bodily functions, though he was speaking at great speed, as if he was in a hurry. Pause. London studio cut to Peter Dimmock in vision who led viewers into the next item.

I let out my breath, which I seemed to have been holding since the start of the race, and had just started to sit back and reflect on my transmission when up came Harry's voice on the special talkback he had to me, which bypassed the main output. 'Alec,' whispered Harry hoarsely, 'I'm on my way. Be ready to leave as soon as I reach the scanner' (the OB van). I slowly started to gather up my papers. This was not what I had in mind. I wanted a drink. I reckoned I deserved a drink. It had gone well and I expected the GRA officials, the owners, to show their appreciation with a drink or two. I was in no hurry to be far away from my scene of triumph. The PA announcer confirmed Harry's correct guess of the winner. A rumbling, dissatisfied noise came from the crowd.

Harry burst into the scanner. 'Quick, quick,' he said, grabbing up the rest of my papers. Just then there was a thunderous knock on the door. 'Quickly,' said Harry again, dashing for the other door at the front of the scanner. 'Harry, Harry. What the hell is all the hurry?' Harry stopped halfway down the steps of the scanner. 'Don't you know what has happened? Let's get just a few yards away from here first of all.'

I followed him quickly through a labyrinth of passageways outside the main stadium stand. 'You really don't, do you? We've been stitched up!' he shouted as he stopped suddenly. He continued, 'That reserve dog. The 18 to 1 outsider. The one in the worst trap, number six. That ugly, untidy, brilliant, bloody awful-looking dog, has won the championship.' There really was distaste for that dog in his voice as he said the last sentence. 'But what is most important of all, for our own skin, we've got to get away from that mob.' So saying he pointed back about 50 yards to where the scanner was parked.

By now there were about 50 to 60 people around the vehicle, mostly men, and they were pushing it from side to side as if to topple it over. It weighed about 5 tons, so I doubt whether they would have completed the task. (I found out a few days later that the senior engineer had locked all the doors, so the eight or nine who remained inside were reasonably safe whilst all this was going on.) 'They reckon the BBC has stitched them up. Most of those have lost hundreds on this race, if not more, and they want blood. Yours and mine to start with.' As Harry was going forth I noticed a police inspector just inside the stadium door. I grabbed him and pointing towards the scanner, told him in a very loud voice that it was a BBC vehicle the crowd were trying to overturn. Within seconds a dozen bobbies were thundering down toward the scene.

We, Harry and I, continued to run in the opposite direction until we were outside the White City Stadium, where we hailed a cab. I sat back, perspiration pouring off me, down my face, inside my shirt, down my trouser legs. This was a completely different experience from the one I had been expecting immediately at the end of the transmission. Red carpet. Champagne. Handshakes. Congratulations from hundreds. 'Christ,' I said more to myself, 'just look at me.' Harry turned just as I blew some of the sweat pouring off the end of my nose. 'Thank your lucky stars it's not your blood pouring down your face. And I thought I knew most of the stings from the boxing game. This will teach you to like dogs.'

Now I know what it's like to be peed on!

A Cat

In my enthusiasm to learn, I acted as stage manager on a live outside broadcast from Chester Zoo, which was being produced by Ray Lakeland. Rehearsal had gone well, except for one thing: a black panther was one of the showpieces of the zoo and all he wanted to do was sleep. The best shot we could get of this huge, fat, lazy, beautiful black cat, was the beast snoring its head off.

'For goodness sake, Alec, do something with that bloody animal. At least get him to open his eyes during transmission, for God's sake.'

Now, I am an animal lover. I understand animals. It was obvious that not the producer, or the commentator, indeed no one, understood this animal like I did. So, just before we went on the air, 15 minutes before we were due to reach the special house featuring our black panther, I slipped away to the restaurant, straight into the kitchens, and talked the chef into giving me a nice big piece of red meat. I got back to our black friend, got a chair and, about six feet from the bars, laid the raw piece of steak on the chair. With luck I felt, in my wisdom and experience, the smell should wake him up and make him slightly less docile.

We went on the air. Now the method of 'shooting' was to direct in a 'leapfrog' style; whilst two cameras were on the parrot house, etc., the other two would be getting 'set up' at the lion house, and so we always used two commentators. Mine at the lion house, where the black panther was housed, was Peter West. I led our team of two cameras and commentator Peter West towards the special house, explaining to him as we went that I had taken steps to ensure that our big cat would not be asleep. I opened the door and went in, and a most extraordinary sight, and sound, greeted us. Our black panther was on its hind legs, stretched up to a height of eight feet, front paws with claws extended, flaying away through the bars trying to get at the out-of-reach steak, roaring its head off as if it were back in the jungle, lips curled back, foam and saliva dripping from its snarling mouth. Ray Lakeland, over talkback from the scanner, said, 'Alec, what the hell have you done? Have you seen the monitors? This is the most ferocious animal ever seen on television. And what is worse, this programme is supposed to entertain children. Millions of kids tonight will have nightmares.'

As I drove toward Liverpool, away from Chester, I'm certain I could still hear my 'big black cat' grumbling in that charming way of his.

A Horse

Once a month I produced a 60-minute programme on World Famous Northern Sportsmen. Fred Perry agreed to participate provided he stayed with us, he was fed up with hotel life. Imagine my

F.J. Perry (Great Britain) in play against G. von Cramm (Germany) whom he beat at Wimbledon in the final of the Men's Singles 1935.   © Hulton Picture Library

40

wife Pamela's shock with my opening remark '...this, my dear, is Fred, Fred Perry, he's staying with us for the next five days...' So, the three times Wimbledon Champion of the 30s showed us both during his stay the friendly north-country charm (he was born in Stockport) that lay underneath that hard core of iron and 'killer' determination.

That was also the main ingredient that propelled Reg Harris through the 40s and 50s. He took to the sport of cycling at the age of eleven but was called into the Army when 19. He served in North Africa in the Tank Corps and when the tank he was driving was hit, it caught fire and Reg was the only survivor. Having been discharged from the forces he quickly regained his fitness, won the world title in '47 and two silver medals in the '48 Olympics. Turning professional the following year, he then won the World Professional Sprint Title four times during the next few years. At the age of 54 he decided to show his third wife, Jennifer, how good he had been, took to the track again and won the British Professional Sprint Title. He announced his retirement in 1975 but, for health reasons continued to have a daily trip of 4/5 miles around the Cheshire lanes and it was

Reg Harris, at the peak of his fame, winning another race at Fallowfield Stadium, Manchester in 1948. © Photocall Manchester

during one of his training spins that he collapsed and died. In the saddle.

When we took our cameras to the Isle of Man to film Geoff Duke reliving his T.T. conquests, little did I realise that this unassuming, quietly spoken champion drove at the Manx corners with half-an-inch to spare at speeds of more than 120 m.p.h. With

Geoff Duke filming for BBC on the Isle of Man with camera, 1959.

Stanley Matthews of Blackpool and England, September 1952 © BBC Hulton Picture Library

our cameras fixed to his handle bars, he demonstrated this time after time. Ice cold nerves.

Which is what Stanley Matthews appeared to have until, under pressure, live on the programme he confessed to being a bag of nerves in the dressing room before any match, be it a lowly league game or an international. He could hardly speak, so to make him feel more 'at home' we had his wife and two children sitting alongside him in the studio. It made a little difference, but not much.

Merryman was the most successful and one of the most enjoyable programmes I worked on, because Merryman II was a horse, a fancied Grand National runner. We filmed in Kelso, Scotland, where he began his racing career. We interviewed his owner, his stable lad and his jockey, Bobby Scott; we showed extracts from his races, and shot a great deal of footage at Neville Crump's training stable at Richmond at 6 in the morning – his gallops over the Yorkshire Downs provided two solid weeks of enjoyable work. I then came up with one of my brilliant ideas: the last five minutes should be live

'*Merryman*', winner of the Grand National, 1960.

from the stables. In the ensuing interview with his trainer, Neville Crump, standing alongside Merryman in the stable yard, the final question asked was, 'So, briefly, Neville, what is it that makes Merryman a great horse?' Neville looked hard at his animal, at his head, his feet, his neck. Then he strode to his rear, slapped him hard on his rump and said, 'That. A bloody great arse.'

There was a pause, a long pause, before I said, 'Run titles.'

It was transmitted, 'arse' and all, two nights before the 1960 Grand National, the first Grand National to be televised live using 10 cameras. Today 39 are used. Incidentally, the race was won by Merryman.

...and The King

The pavement was damp, the wind was whistling around the station and certainly around one's ankles and legs, causing bouts of foot stomping to keep warm. I pulled my coat collar closer around my neck. Stations were definitely one of the coldest places to be in January, and Manchester's Piccadilly was no exception. I was up by the ticket gate of platform four just after twelve, and the London train was due in a few minutes. The place smelt as if steam trains were still running, a pungent mixture of coal, tar and dampness, and on a miserable day like this it seemed to get deep into one's lungs.

As I stamped I was aware of a lot of activity from half a dozen or so railway porters: two were running out a long piece of corded carpet from alongside me at the ticket gate to roughly where the engine came to a standstill; a couple more were brushing the carpet, and some were shouting for someone to collect their uniformed caps and jackets. They increased their activity and panic just when the nose of the train appeared from the direction of Stockport. Obviously, one of 'the royals' was expected, or perhaps the Lord Mayor of Manchester. Had Matt Busby reached the dizzy heights of a red carpet?

The huge diesel came to a halt without any fuss with the front first-class door coming to a standstill right in line with the front of the red carpet. Our half-dozen 'flunkies', as I mentally labelled them, lined up either side of the front first-class door. The driver, too, quickly dropped out of his cab, straightened his tie and put on the special shiny train-driver's cap. I tore my eyes away to look for my own particular guest, the former World Snooker Champion, Joe Davis – champion from 1927 through to 1947 – by then doing TV and exhibition work. He was my, the BBC's, guest in Manchester for the next couple of days whilst I produced a match into *Grandstand* between Joe and brother Fred Davis. This match would decide the winner of the Grandstand Snooker Championship. 'Now, listen, Alec,' London's *Grandstand* editor, Paul Fox, had said a couple of days earlier, 'Joe is to win this, it's all arranged.' So here at Manchester Piccadilly, the small group of 'flunkies' stiffly straightened to come to some form of attention. There, stepping down into their midst was my man, Joe Davis. He nodded to all in turn, slipping something into the hand of the last member with the most gold brocade on his hat, this being the stationmaster, who fell into step alongside Joe, who himself had started down the red carpet. His actions were all so very natural and came so easy after years of practice, just raising his left hand in acknowledgement to the occasional shout, cheer, applause. Cream-coloured shammy leather gloves, matching his camel-haired coat with the thick dark-brown fur collar. He seemed to glide down the red carpet with the chattering baboons behind him, each carrying a portion of his luggage. When Joe was about 20 yards from the gate I stepped forward. For a couple of seconds a look of horror filled the stationmaster's face. 'Hello, Joe, it's Alec Weeks,' I said, walking forward, hand outstretched. A big grin lightened the great man's features. He took my hand in both of his, looking up, but at the same time this little man's rotund five-foot-six figure seemed huge. A big man in many ways, I was beginning to realise.

I guided Joe to where our limousine was parked. The driver was already standing to attention with the rear door open, cap in hand. I laughed quietly to myself. I had arranged for the hired car to collect me, take me to the station and then remain with Joe until he returned on the London train tomorrow evening. When earlier I had got into the car, which was a huge ostentatious limousine, I just couldn't help myself: 'What the hell have you got this for? Joe's not getting married, but this is big enough and fit for the Queen.' Of course the hire-car company knew who they would be driving around. As I sank into the beautifully cushioned leather upholstery I thought, 'Good enough for a King – King Joe Davis'.

All this pomp and glory was continued when we arrived at the Grand Hotel. I had been alerted by *Grandstand* in London that Joe never stayed at any other hotel in Manchester except The Grand. I do not know how it was done, and never will, but as we drew up outside the hotel, the front staff were already lined up either side of the steps, with the manager, Basil Thornton, standing at the top of the marbled steps to the massive front doors, which were already held open by two flunkies. We were led to the lift by Thornton. 'Come on up, Alec,' said Joe. We had already agreed to have lunch together. 'We'll have a drink before we go down.'

'You have your usual suite, Mr Davis,' offered Thornton. 'I've also taken the liberty of putting on ice the hotel's complimentary bottle of champagne, Bollinger '55, which you always prefer, Mr Davis.' Someone took Joe's coat and gloves. 'Leave your wardrobe to us, Mr Davis,' Thornton said while he opened and poured out two lovely, ample glasses of Bollinger '55.

The adulation continued into lunch. A round table for six in the centre of the restaurant had been relaid for two, and at least eight waiters of varying seniority hovered and fluttered. They left us with the menu for at least five minutes whilst Joe and I talked of this and that, diving back to the menu every so often. 'Recommend the plaice, Alec. There is nowhere in the UK that can beat their plaice.' With that the head waiter dived in with, 'I can recommend the lobster bisque, Mr Davis. Not on the menu, of course.' And so it went on, a bottle of light Mosel to start with, and 'your favourite claret, Mr Davis, with your chateaubriand.' I had plaice, but I would have eaten anything as long as I could have seen and heard this floor show. Six waiters then hovered around us throughout lunch, just out of earshot. 'My God, Joe, you are certainly well liked up here.' 'My stamping ground,' replied Joe. 'This is where it all started.' Then during our lunch he proceeded to paint me a fascinating picture of the early days.

Though born in a Nottinghamshire mining town, he grew up in Chesterfield, where his father ran a pub (later the Queen's Hotel), which had a full-size billiard table. There, at the age of 11, Joe took up billiards and snooker, encouraged by his father. Challenge matches by and to a 11/12-year-old always drew a crowd that spent money. At the age of 13 he turned professional and won the Chesterfield championship. From then on he was playing in all the major Northern cities: Newcastle, Leeds, Sheffield, Manchester and Liverpool. By the early 30s Joe had built up a fantastic following. When money became short during the depression, Joe took the game abroad to countries like South Africa, Australia, New Zealand, taking on all comers. During the war Joe toured all the camps in Britain, entertaining the troops as only Joe knew how.

I departed about 4.30 p.m., leaving Joe in the hands of the wine waiter, who had just produced his favourite Havana cigar. I knew 'King Joe' would be safe for the evening, and we were due to meet at the BBC Television Studios, Dickenson Road, about 12 noon the following day.

I had been rehearsing the various shots for about an hour when, at 11.30 a.m., brother Fred Davis arrived. He was about five years younger than Joe, of the same rotund build and the same height of five-six, glasses, but not very similar in looks. Quietly spoken, he quickly shed his outer clothes and, screwing together his cue, was soon practising away. Joe appeared bang on the button of noon, nodded and bid good day to most in the studio, went up and hugged his brother and beckoned me over. After shaking my hand and asking how I was he went on, 'We know exactly what Paul [Fox] wants, Alec. If you can just tell us a minute before we go on the

46

air, fine, but otherwise an accurate two minutes before you want us to stop. Leave everything to us. You just concentrate on those nice pictures. Anything you want you just tell us, OK.'

Grandstand went on the air at 1 o'clock. Joe and Fred reappeared, this time in their immaculate evening dress 'our working clothes', as Fred called them. Our scene-setter from Manchester consisted of Joe and Fred tossing up. Fred having won then elected to start the game and off they went. Four visits approximately twenty minutes each followed during the afternoon, during which Fred won the first frame and Joe won the next. Fred was due to start the last and deciding frame. This would 'settle' the Grandstand Snooker Tournament. They came over for the last visit about ten past four. Now, as you know, I had been told, very, very confidentially, that Joe would be winning this match.

Joe started off in this final frame with the score at a frame each. After Joe had made a break of about nine, Fred took the cue ball and made 10. Then Joe took it again, scored only a single point and then lost it to Fred. Terrific snooker, terribly exciting, but I was beginning to get just a little concerned. Fred held the cue ball and was slowly building up a score: he had got to 32 and was going strong. The phone rang: It was Paul Fox: 'Alec, tell Joe he's got two minutes!' Now I realised this great editor in London had forgotten the plan. He must be mad, he couldn't possibly know anything about snooker. 'But Paul,' I blustered, 'Fred has the table and Joe is about 20 behind.' 'Alec,' said Paul in a slightly louder voice, 'get a message, a signal, through to Joe to tell him he's got two minutes left.' 'But Paul...' I started. This time Paul Fox not only shouted down the phone, he pressed the talkback key and said, 'Tell Joe he's got two minutes left.' He shouted this so loudly that anyone in Salford, three miles away, would have heard. Joe and Fred down on the studio floor certainly did.

Through some extreme piece of 'bad luck' Fred played a miss-hit and lost the cue ball. One minute and fifty-five seconds left.

Little Joe Davis took the cue ball. What followed was something I will never forget in my whole life.

ONE MINUTE AND FORTY-FIVE SECONDS LEFT. He started with the reds – ZIP, ZAP, THUD, PLOP, SWISH, AND ZAP, BOOM, WALLOP, AND ANOTHER ZIP – potting a colour in between each one. All reds gone from the table. All

Joe Davis, king of snooker, February 1962.

Joe had to do was to clear all the colours off the table. That was all.

ONE MINUTE LEFT. The coloured balls were all over the table. The yellow: 52 seconds left. The brown: 45 seconds. The green: 32 seconds. The blue: 20 seconds. The pink: 11 seconds.

Now the black, with the white cue ball in one corner, the black in the other. Pause, crack, straight in! Two seconds left.

Joe Davis had won the rubber and the 'championship'.

Paul Fox on the talkback: 'Alec, you were magnificent. Well done.' I felt a fraud. I looked down into the studio. Joe was surrounded by cameramen, electricians, sound technicians, all trying to shake his hand. Fred was opening a bottle of bubbly.

Before he left the studio and after *Grandstand* had come off air, Joe had spoken to Paul on the phone. All I heard of the conversation was Joe quietly chuckling into the mouthpiece. I was pleased with my efforts. The direction had gone OK.

I travelled with Joe and Fred to Manchester Piccadilly to catch the London-bound express. Lightly placing his hand on my arm, Joe said, 'Remember, Alec, always leave it to us. No matter what the sport. You concentrate on your pretty pictures.' I remembered those words and did just that throughout the whole of my television career. When they got on the train all the old razzmatazz started all over again: the bowing, saluting, standing to attention, cheering, the red carpet and the worshipping into their seats. To be honest, it had never really stopped.

As the train slowly left the station carrying the one and only Joe Davis and his brother Fred, two attendants were helping them out of their coats and the head waiter was offering them a bottle of Bollinger '55.

Chapter Four

A Pugnacious Chapter

Boxing is not everyone's cup of tea! But whenever two men fight, and they will, a crowd will gather. When a crowd gathers, money will change hands, and men will fight for money.

He left the dressing room and its odours of embrocation and sweat. The noise coming from the arena resembled the sound of an approaching tube train. He prepared himself for the effect of the first deep breath of 'the fight crowd', its rancid mixture of cigar and cigarette smoke always got deep inside him, making his throat dry, mouth parched and his eyes water at the blue haze that hung over the noisy packed stadium.

He started to move down the aisle, through the crowds who were standing chatting, some saw him and stood back, making way and shouting at him at the same time. 'Good luck, laddie!' Faces offered advice: '...I've got a fiver on you ... watch his head...' '...I'm on you to go the distance'.

His mind by now was focusing on the illuminated square ahead of him. What the smiling, snarling, shouting faces uttered didn't register, coarse and blasphemous at the top, milder as he moved forward into the ringside area.

He reached the ring. Already he could feel the warmth of the arc lamps, their heat cutting short the haze of smoke, making it clear inside the roped area. He bounded up the four steps, ducked under the top rope, jigged into the centre, and raised an arm. For just a split second the babble ceased, the crowd hushed. Someone clapped, a dog barked. The babble started up all over again.

He moved over to a neutral corner and thoroughly shuffled his fight boots in the resin.

He moved to his corner, Blue Corner. His corner man was down talking to someone. He looked up, came up the steps and nodded. He took the gum-shield from his fighter's clenched, gloved fist, putting it in the bucket of water by the ring seat. He started to knead and massage his fighter's shoulders under the towel.

The opponent arrived wearing a flashy red and white gown. He had three corner men with him, all talked loudly, laughing falsely at some lame joke. Their 'charge' just kept his head down, shuffling his feet.

The MC climbed into the ring, reaching for the microphone.

'Ladies and gentlemen. This is a middleweight contest over six three-minute rounds. Between, in the blue corner...'

The announcement brought forth very little applause but the crowd acknowledged the start of another bout by changing to a loud murmur as they moved and settled in their seats. The betting boys took the opportunity of making a quick 'killing' by shouting out attractive odds.

The referee climbed up into the ring. He raised his arms, signalling the two fighters and the corner men to the centre of the ring. He looked at the gloves of each fighter, then said, 'I want this to be a clean fight...'

He looked at his opponent's two-day stubble around the chin, thinking 'He'll use that in the clinches.'

'When I tell you to break, you break, cleanly...' He noticed the flattened nose, the big wad of Vaseline over the left eyebrow. 'No illegal use of the head or elbows...'

His opponent was 2–3 inches shorter, he was muscular around the neck and shoulders. He was a fighter, not a boxer.

'Now shake hands...'

They touched gloves. His opponent had still to look him in the eye.

'Go back to your corners and come out at the bell.'

He returned to his corner. He knew he would win, it was just a question of 'how' and 'when'.

The crowd became, to him, a distant murmur. 'Clang'. His corner man patted him twice on the shoulder and pushed him to the centre of the ring. His opponent weaved towards him. He felt the warm arcs bring out the perspiration on his forehead. This was the loneliest place on earth.

In most of our lives there is one certain something, or someone, that helps to change the course of one's life. I remember very clearly indeed what that something was in my life.

My progress in the world of amateur boxing was quick, but in the RAF it really took off. Every station was forever staging a boxing tournament, and it was in two of these I was to meet a talented young boxer named Randolph Turpin. Hailing from Leamington Spa, he was a year younger than myself but virtually undefeated in the amateur ranks. Why I thought I could beat him I do not know. We met first of all at RAF Cardington then two months later at RAF Wisbech. Randy won on both occasions. He had a punch like a mule. After that second meeting we spent several hours together waiting for our transport and sitting around in the sergeants' mess.

Randy talked boxing most of the time; in fact we both did. He certainly knew the history of the sport. That was in 1945. The following year Randy turned pro and rapidly climbed the ladder, finally in 1951 beating the 'invincible' Sugar Ray Robinson for the World Middleweight title. This bout took place at Earls Court, and virtually the whole of London came to a standstill that evening between the time of half past eight and ten o'clock. Taxis were parked, nose to tail either side, the length of Regent Street. What a fight! What a win!

So, Randy Turpin was World Champion and expected full recognition in every way, such as a fee for being interviewed. Today that right is recognised, and sportsmen receive fees of thousands of pounds for each interview. In the dark ages of 1951 this was not so, and the BBC was very much inclined to treat all sportsmen and sportswomen as if they were gentlemen from Oxford or Cambridge University and the word 'money' should not taint the conversation. At this time, the '50s, the Beeb had a terrible reputation for small, or no, payments. So after a few weeks of giving interviews Randy put his foot down and said no to all interviews. This ban went on for weeks and weeks. Famous broadcasters tried to talk Randy round to be interviewed, but with no luck. Raymond Glendenning, Alan Clarke, John Snagge. No. No. No. One day at

53

one of the outside-broadcast departmental meetings which I was privileged to attend – providing I sat at the back! – I spoke up and said I would have a go at getting an interview with Randolph Turpin. I was scoffed at. Laughed at. Ridiculed. But, more as a giggle than anything else, I would be allowed to try to get an interview with Randy for the famous Raymond Glendenning.

At that time Randy was appearing on stage at the Trocadero Theatre, Elephant & Castle, in an exhibition of training, sparring, etc., that was playing to packed houses. The lad was popular and the money was pouring in. So down we went in a recording car: the recording engineer, Raymond Glendenning, and myself. I left the other two in the car and went up to the stage door. I told the doorman my name, where I was from and who I wanted to see, ending with, 'Tell Randy, it's Sergeant Alec Weeks from the RAF.' The doorman disappeared and a few minutes later Randy's elder brother Dick appeared and beckoned me. I followed him through a few corridors into a dressing room and there was Randy Turpin with a big grin on his face, and he gave me a lovely big warm hug. A few marks and scars now dotted his face and eyebrows, but his eyes, and big toothy smile were just as young as ever.

After we had dispensed with the hellos and the small talk about the past, I found him still very modest about his fantastic achievement. Then I remembered my two colleagues outside in the car and reluctantly explained what I wanted and that he would be doing me a personal favour if he would grant us an interview to be conducted by Raymond Glendenning. He was silent for a few moments then said, 'I'll agree on two conditions, that I am paid £5 cash, and that I am only granting this interview because of a favour to Alec Weeks.' I dashed out and told Raymond. When the interview was done Randy told Glendenning, 'If any further interviews are required by the BBC for radio or television, they must all be arranged through Alec Weeks. When he contacts me, I will say yes or no.' Now, this was a complete surprise to me; we hadn't discussed or arranged this, and as he said it Randy turned to me and winked. Raymond mumbled something about passing his message on to the BBC authorities, and he did just that very soon after we returned. Of course, no one paid any attention. But after a few days with no one else getting anywhere the penny dropped. I was asked by this programme or that programme to arrange for this with Randy or that with Randy. I contacted him on his special

Randolph Turpin having a workout, December 1949.

number and got a yes or no. Nearly all the time he only asked for a five-pound fee. Imagine what today's 'sporting stars' would request. I don't think it dawned upon the people in power at the BBC what a bargain they were getting, but what did happen was my prestige grew overnight. I was previously known within a very small working circle of BBC radio. Within a month of Randy's demand every programme department had heard of me, and as 90 per cent of their requests were granted by Randy, and because of the very reasonable fee, my name become known throughout the Beeb. This enabled me to put my foot on the first rung of that elusive ladder, and it was all due to Randolph Turpin and me getting to know each other in the ring at RAFs Cardington and Wisbech six years earlier.

Speaking of boxers, one name that will always spring to mind is little Peter Kane, World Flyweight Champion from 1938 until 1943. In Manchester I thought of the idea of doing a series of programmes about famous northern sportsmen of yesteryear, and after several

55

weeks, Peter Kane was tracked down to an address in Widnes, just outside the Pilkington Glassworks where he then worked. I only had the address, no phone number, so one evening I drove across to Widnes, or Lowton, to be exact, just outside Widnes. His place was in the middle of a long row of two-up two-down terraced houses, and had certainly been built for the workers at the glassworks. I knocked on the door of number 5. The outside of the terraced house certainly needed a coat of paint. The door opened and standing there was the legend. One of the greatest flyweights of our time. Still very recognisable from his famous days in the '30s, which by then were twenty years earlier. There were dark rings under his eyes and his stubble made him look like a hedgehog – he'd needed a shave yesterday. I introduced myself. We shook hands and I explained what I had in mind. He invited me in to save us from standing on the doorstep for what was obviously going to be a lengthy discussion. Walking on threadbare lino, the little fellow led me past grimy wallpaper into a room at the rear of the house. The original cream paint of the doors was now chipped and dark yellow. The lounge, parlour, call it what you will, consisted of a kitchen table with one leg propped up by an orange box. There was also a deckchair with no material, just thick string stretched across the frame tightly enough to sit on. A grimy plastic radio stood on the shelf of the built-in larder. And that was it. Nothing on the tatty, filthy walls, no pictures, no paintings, no photos of great years. He apologised for the state of things. His wife, he said, had left him some time ago and he hadn't had time to get organised. Our conversation mainly consisted of talking about money. He originally asked for a lot. When I started to take my leave with a 'let me think about it' type of comment, he dropped his asking price immediately. We finally agreed on a figure. After all, it was going to be a 30-minute programme just about Peter, and I did want to get the best out of him. Though we agreed on the fee of £150 (this was 1960, and that was a good fee for the day), I wouldn't agree to any advance payments. This started a succession of phone calls. Every day he rang me asking for an advance. Eventually, I finally agreed to a one-third advance, £50, a week before the show.

On the afternoon of the transmission from the BBC's Dickenson Road Studios, Peter arrived for afternoon rehearsal, dressed in a sports shirt, slightly sweat-marked, and a pair of scruffy jeans. He said he had a change for the transmission. We ran through all the library material of his fights and the interviews with others who had taken part in his boxing life. We rehearsed. Peter Kane looked, and at times sounded, like an ex-champion, someone down on his luck, someone whose faculties were all working but who had definitely seen better days. The stagehands, the cameramen, all liked him. He seemed difficult to dislike. We broke two hours before the 9.15 transmission. Peter went into his dressing room 'to relax'. I had some sandwiches and coffee sent into him. Make-up went in and just dabbed any shiny patches. Still an hour to go. I ran through a few points with my vision mixer. Fifteen minutes to go. Get everyone on set. Everyone ready for transmission.

The stage manager went to Peter's dressing room, which was at the rear of the studios. Out came a man, a person I had only seen in the newspapers or on the newsreel. He was dressed from head to foot in evening dress with an immaculate white shirt and black bow tie, jacket and trousers beautifully pressed, the lapels finished in lovely silk, his black patent shoes squeaking slightly and the whole effect finished on the top with immaculate Brylcreem-combed hair. This was not the ex-fighter, but Peter Kane, the former world champion. A lot of difference. He seemed taller. He walked upright and his performance during the programme was perfection. The 45 minutes went by in no time, and Peter enthused over every shot of library material, never hesitating, as if it was only yesterday when it had all taken place. He astounded everyone, especially myself.

I was trying to recall the scruffy individual I had first met a couple of months ago. We had a few drinks afterwards, all the participants within the programme. This was what Peter had wanted his advance for: to go out and hire a dinner suit and dress up as he had when he was the World Champion. Mentally and emotionally, that attire really did turn the clock back twenty years or so. A car was organised to take him home and, as he left the studios, he tipped the two commissionaires standing at the door, just like a World Champion would do, though he hardly had two pennies to rub together. But this was the great Peter Kane. His performance was so good, a little 'bonus' was sent his way a few weeks later.

I will never forget that time when, for just an hour or so, the crowd roared again for this great sportsman.

* * *

Jock McAvoy of Rochdale, April 1938.
© BBC Hulton Picture Library

Jock McAvoy. British Middle-weight Champion from 1933 until 1944, also Light Heavy-weight Champion from 1937 to 1938. Jock started fighting in the 1920s on the cobbled streets of his home town of Rochelle for two shillings and six-pence a fight. He really came up the hard way. He retired in 1944, but in the late '40s was stricken down with polio. By the early '50s he was getting himself around on crutches, calipers, wheelchair, etc. Throughout the late '50s he could be found on Blackpool's Golden Mile guessing people's weights. From 1958 onwards he lived in a large caravan just outside Sale, south of Manchester, supervising the letting of spaces on the site. I got him in for a 30-minute programme. There was masses of library material, and he was a good talker, but there was one question and answer I will never, ever forget.

'Jock, throughout your boxing career you must have been one of the fittest men in the country, yet you went down with polio. How did you keep your sanity for such an active man?'

'Alec, when I was at my peak, in the thirties, I lived life to the full and I was a very naughty boy. Wine, women, song, gambling. You name it, I did it, had it, even in the dressing room before or after a fight. I knew that one day I would have to pay for it, and this is it,' he said, tapping his two dead legs. 'But life is still great. I am moving around in third gear now and am seeing a lot more of the world and life than I did in the heyday. I have time to take it all in nowadays.'

I found that a fantastic philosophical outlook on his present life. No complaints or moans about how life had treated him. He just accepted it. That was in 1960. He died in 1965.

58

*   *   *

Whenever two men fight, a crowd will gather. And they were certainly gathering on that night on the Piccadilly Line tube train. It was about 7.15 p.m. and although the West End rush hour was over, the train was packed, standing room only, and smoke-laden; the metallic humming of wheels on track was lost in the hubbub, the chat going on in all the carriages. Everyone was talking to everyone else. Fight talk. The mainly male occupants were arguing, discussing, shouting the odds over this fighter or that one. Some looked as if they had come straight from Covent Garden Market or Billingsgate, some from the City. Here and there a well-dressed enthusiast would be offering his opinion, with the *Financial Times* in one hand and in the other, holding on tightly, his son or his nephew, about 10 or 11, being taken to 'the fights' – perhaps for the first time. Sitting, lounging, would be the ex-pros. Some had eyebrows thickened with scar tissue, others with their noses broadened, or an occasional screwed-up ear; all listening to one another, nodding their heads, which rested on thick muscular necks, sometimes even offering a short opinion: 'But a fraction before he throws his right he will drop his left guard'. For a second or two those around him would stop jabbering: the words of wisdom from an expert must be accepted, never ignored. Indeed, if they had a bearing on one of the fights that night his words would be quoted for weeks to come. And so it went on, and on, through station after station until, as the journey began to reach its end, the chattering, the jabbering, the comments reached a higher and higher pitch. We were nearly there.

One third of all this noisy gathering were in their late twenties or thirties, the ex-servicemen, those who had disappeared as boys in 1939 and reappeared as hardened men six years later. Though some were four sails to the wind, they still had their faculties and joined in the nostalgia, though they could only speak of the pre-war greats. 'My dad took me to see Len Harvey when he was heavyweight champ.' 'Benny Lynch was the greatest fighter ever to leave Scottish shores.' These lads had done their fighting and tonight they would see other professionals at work. They still had some of their demob money to play with, and from 1945 all the big sporting events had been pulling gigantic crowds: soccer, athletics, speedway, dog and horse racing, but none more so than a big fight

59

night – and they didn't come any bigger than the Jack Solomon Promotion at Harringay Arena.

Up the escalator and out into the fresh air above, and the world of noise really began to open up. The newspaper vendors were shouting the odds, all seeming to cluster around the various exits. Then, just behind them, the spivs – 'Have you got any tickets?' 'Good money for good tickets' 'Who wants to buy tickets for the big fight?' – dozens and dozens of them, all the way from the tube station to the arena, and I swear, though I always heard the words clearly, I never, ever saw their lips move.

The roads and pavements were awash with people, all moving slowly in the right direction. No one was hurrying, or panicking; that would come in an hour and a half, when the time for the main bout was approaching. For now this journey was one to savour, to enjoy, and above all to remember. On the very edges of the pavements the market men were selling souvenir postcards of some of the well-known fighters, or cheap books and articles of their careers. Every so often a bible-pusher would be shouting, 'Repent thee thy sins, said the Lord' or 'Fight the good fight with Jesus'. 'Do you hear the voice of Jesus?' 'No,' shouts a wag, 'only Eamonn Andrews on BBC.' Whatever, it always brought forth a good few wisecracks from the cockney wags.

As one got closer, Harringay appeared well illuminated, and the crowds began to thin as they split to enter their own doors around the arena. The mounted police gently kept you moving in an orderly fashion. They were there just to help, there was never trouble from a fight crowd. And this was some crowd.

As one got near to the turnstiles the bell for the early prelim fight could be heard. The promotion had started at 7.30 p.m., but no one bothered about the first fight of the evening, which was generally watched by a man and a dog. One stood around talking about the bigger fights to come, whilst the cigarette and cigar smoke began to build up and pollute the air with its fumes. The betting boys, just a few rows behind ringside, were beginning to warm up. Excitement rippled through one's body, the hairs on the back of the neck prickled.

Tonight was the night for the British Heavyweight Champion, Bruce Woodcock. He came from the drab streets of a Yorkshire mining town, a pitman's son. The 27-year-old fighter was a people's favourite who had learnt his trade in the amateur ranks whilst

60

Britain's heavyweight hope, Bruce Woodcock, December 1946. © BBC Hulton Picture Library

earning his living as a fitter in the Doncaster LNER railway works. He had captured the hearts of all and sundry when taking on the burly heavyweight champion Jack London at Tottenham Hotspur Football Club in July 1945. The war in Germany had just finished, and Woodcock took the title with a sixth-round knockout. He fought his way from poverty to riches. The people loved him. He won fight after fight. He could box, had a lovely left hand and a hell of a dig with his right. He was virtually in line for a title fight with the World Champion, Joe Louis, providing he could get past tonight's obstacle in the form of an American bruiser from Detroit named Joe Baksi. Now, Baksi was a rough, tough fighter. Only a few months earlier (in the previous November), he had stopped our own light heavyweight champion, Freddy Mills, in six rounds. But Freddy had been giving away a lot of weight, said the so-called experts.

The proof that fight fever had hit London was the fact that at midday at the weigh-in at Jack Solomon's gym, opposite the Windmill Theatre, the crowds that flocked there had brought Piccadilly Circus to a standstill for two hours solid. By 9.15 p.m., when the two fighters entered the ring, one could feel the tension, the excitement, in that hot, smoky arena. The fight had not yet started, yet the crowd were already roaring, stamping their feet. Baksi was first into the ring, to be followed within a minute by the northern lad. The American shuffled in his corner whilst he was being gloved up, with Woodcock dancing and jigging around. It is said that when the two fighters were finally introduced to the crowd the roar that greeted the British Champion could be heard five miles away.

Referee Moss Deyong instructed the fighters. They touched gloves. Then back to their corners, robes and dressing gowns removed by

Bruce Woodcock, British Heavyweight champion 1945–1950, works on the speed bag during training. © EMPICS

their trainers, mouthpieces in, a quick rub of more Vaseline by Baksi's trainer, Ray Arcel. Tom Hurst was stroking away at Woodcock's muscles. Both fighters were now looking straight across at each other. The hatred was there. The bell went. For just a couple of seconds the crowd were still, then the roar broke again like a wave. Woodcock was quickly moving around the ring, flitting out his rapier left lead, landing well with 50 per cent of them. The American just shuffled forward, bobbing, weaving, swaying, trying to avoid Woodcock's leads and landing now and again with stiff jabs to the body. The round was two and a half minutes old and was definitely going the Englishman's way. Then Baksi brought over a light swinging left to the side of Woodcock's head. Woodcock momentarily appeared just to ride the punch, which seemed so light and uneventful. Then it flattened him as if he had been poleaxed. He was on his back in the centre of the ring when the bell went to signify the end of the round, and his manager, Tom Hurst, and his seconds, dragged him to his corner. He recovered during the minute break and for the next five rounds even attempted to outbox the American. But he was in a terrible mess, blood continually spraying out from his mouth and nose as he threw punches. The right side of his face was just getting larger and larger, and his eye was disappearing inside a swollen mess of mussy skin. Referee Deyong stopped the fight in Baksi's favour in the seventh round.

The bubble had burst. Another British heavyweight had been beaten by an American. The thousands and thousands at the

Harringay Arena that night went quietly home, shaken, subdued, not only disenchanted with the fight game, but saddened for their hero.

That was 15th April 1947. Turn the clock forward to October 1959 and the BBC's Television Studios at Dickenson Road,

Author directing in Manchester, 1959

Manchester. I had been producing, just for BBC northern viewers, a 60-minute programme on famous northern sportsmen of the past – people such as Reg Harris, Geoff Duke, Stanley Matthews and Fred Perry – and thought I would like to do something on Woodcock. So that October evening, having phoned earlier to make an appointment to see Bruce, I drove over to the outskirts of Doncaster, to an estate of lovely large neo-Tudor houses, all detached. I walked up the path of the address I had. Norma, Bruce's wife, opened the door and welcomed me in the way that true northerners have, with warmth and friendliness. She showed me into the study and to Bruce. He, likewise, was friendly, and after the usual formalities, and once I felt that Bruce was relaxed, I outlined the type of programme I wanted to do, using him and his manager Tom Hurst to take me through his career and into quite a lot of his fights. He

63

was very reluctant over the whole idea. Polite, but not at all keen. I tried to emphasise the simplicity of the whole programme, but that made it even worse.

'Sorry. I've made up my mind. No. I won't do it.' Sweating inwardly, I still struggled along. 'You know, Bruce, I can remember your fights as if they were yesterday, but do you know it's getting on for ten years since you were packing 'em in? A hell of a lot of people think you're dead!' Bruce looked hard at me for some seconds. 'On the level?' 'Bruce, I told my boss this morning that I was coming over to see you and his comment was that you must have emigrated or died.' He was silent. Just looking at me. I also remained quiet, for once. 'OK. That does it. I'll appear, but I insist my son, young Bruce, sits in your control room, or somewhere he can see everything that's going on. I want him to see what life is like, not just in television, but in the fight game.'

I later found the reason behind those strange last few words, 'what life's like in the fight game'. Shortly afterwards Norma brought in the coffee and offered to show me around their home. It was expensively, but tastefully, furnished, a home of comfort and well-being. Nowhere in the house was there anything whatsoever to show that the head of the household had been entangled for 15 years in the hardest, bloodiest sport of all.

As Bruce later said on the programme, 'I kidded the children. [He had two, a boy and a girl.] I told them I had been hit by a steamroller. They never knew I had been a fighter until 1954, when Harringay Arena closed and on its last night all the champions were introduced from the ring. The occasion was televised live. And that was the first time the children learned I had been heavyweight champion.'

His face, the left side, carried just a moon-shaped scar above the eye, but his right side carried many battle scars, especially around his eye. Indeed the right eye itself would, towards the end of the day, move slowly out of alignment, and so on the night of the programme, an hour before transmission, he sat for 30 minutes or so in a darkened room.

During the weeks preceding the programme I had selected many clips of Bruce's fights, those against Gus Lesnevich, Freddie Mills, Jack London and, of course, the one against Joe Baksi – the one that turned Woodcock's career. Tom Hurst had been Bruce's manager and still lived, not only in Manchester, but in Dickenson Road, where our studios were. I talked him into coming on to the programme, and we arranged to spend a morning a few days later in the studio viewing room, looking at our selected clips from Woodcock's fights. So just the two of us sat thoroughly enjoying ourselves, Tom reliving those great fights, until the Baksi fight: then he sat forward on the edge of his seat, hands clenched, and after 10 minutes perspiration was running down his face. 'Could we see the Baksi fight again?' Three times I had the same request. Three times we repeated the film. 'A great one I've got here,' I thought. 'He's gone loopy.' 'Is there a machine [by which] we can see the punch and knock-down in the first round, but in slow motion?' Tom asked after the third showing.

I arranged for the projectionist to rerun this on one of our editing machines. We watched this sorry historic disaster again, this time in slow motion. When the machine stopped, Tom, without a word, led me back into the viewing room. We were quite alone.

'I know, lad, you know something about boxing.' I nodded. 'So tell me, how can a left swing, delivered with the inside of the glove, and leading with the left foot, break – no smash – the upper part of the temporal bone of a jawbone, and part of a cheek, into little pieces?' The injuries were quite correct. The examining doctor at Charing Cross Hospital had only once seen a fracture as bad as this, and then the patient had been hit by a sledgehammer! 'At least,' said the doctor, 'whoever did this smashed his hand up.' But Baksi hadn't.

'How,' continued Tom, 'how can a gentle swing, landed with the inside of a padded glove, do so much damage? How can a padded thumb break the thickest bone in Bruce's face?'

That fight happened 12 years earlier, but I had only been in television for a few months and lacked the courage, the nerve to broadcast manager Tom Hurst's version.

The programme went off very well, Bruce's Yorkshire dialect bringing a warmth and naturalness to the programme. In answer to the Baksi sucker punch Bruce said, 'We had only been going a couple of minutes and Baksi stood in front of me, making a few loose probing swings with his left hand. I could see he was in no way fixed to put any power into a left swing, and I remember thinking to myself, he's gambling on a quick right. So it looked, and to test this theory I half-led with my left to see if Baksi's hand was starting. At that moment Baksi pulled over his sucker punch.

65

It landed on the side of my head – and the effect was the same as if he'd thrown half a ton of lead weight at me! My brain became numb. My legs, arms, head, all seemed to be leaving me. Baksi's bulk became like a vague, ghostly vision in front of me. I couldn't see properly. The whole vast arena seemed to be swimming around me in a crazy whirlpool of lights and heads and white shirts, like a trick camera shot from a Hollywood film trailer. I lost all sense of balance and distance, all count of time. I don't remember going down, but Tom Hurst says I was on my back, looking vaguely up at the roof, when the bell marked the end of the first round. He picked me up and half-carried, half-dragged me back to the corner...'

And in reply to the final question, 'So, briefly, Bruce, in this famous career, what is your proudest, your greatest moment?'

'When my boy passed his 11-plus examination to the grammar school. I realised then it had all been worth it.'

In spite of everything Bruce Woodcock had achieved and everything he had experienced, in spite of all the pain, it was the simple things in life that gave him his greatest pleasure. As the closing titles of the programme were running I felt very, very humble.

When I look at that fight again – and I have done, dozens of times – I still wonder about the rumours that abounded about that Baksi fight.

Just close your left hand into a fist, holding the knuckle downward. Now swing your hand up so that the knuckle of the thumb connects with a hard object. Hurts, doesn't it? Remember, the thickest bone in the face. 'No padded glove did this,' said a hospital doctor. 'It must have been a sledgehammer or a steamroller.'

'What do you think?'

Freddie Mills. Now there was a fighter! World Light Heavyweight Champion from 1948 to 1950. He started his professional career in 1936 in his home town of Bournemouth, when 17 years old. That career lasted 14 years, during which time he had 96 professional fights and won British, Empire, European and, finally, World titles. There were some horrible, hard fights, yet he seemed to have finished his fighting career with his senses all intact. A wealthy man, he switched to the 'boards' after his retirement in 1950, and appeared on the stage in farces, pantomimes, circuses. He just loved

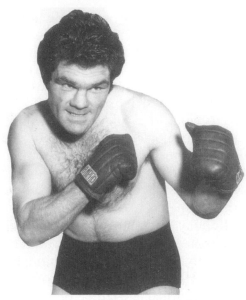

Freddie Mills, January 1950.
© BBC Hulton Picture Library

a crowd, cheering and especially laughing.

I first met him in the RAF when I sparred with him at some RAF exhibition. He treated me gently. I was to spar with him on other occasions after that, the last time being in January 1950 at Windsor, when he was training and preparing for his World Championship defence against the American Joey Maxim. He lost and retired. Our paths crossed during my career in sports broadcasting, first in radio then television.

World Light Heavyweight champion Freddie Mills sparring with the author prior to defence of title, January 1950. © BBC Hulton Picture Library

We often had dinner together with our respective wives. He was a good host.

In 1960 he opened up a Chinese Restaurant just off Tottenham Court Road. It did fairly good business – well, he certainly wasn't losing on the venture. He worked at the restaurant business. It wasn't just a pastime. He would generally arrive about 5 o'clock in the evening and leave about 3 o'clock the following morning. About 9.30/10 he would always pop out around the back of the restaurant for an hour or so 'before the theatres and cinemas closed for the night' for a quick 'shut-eye'. He often told me that a snatched hour or two of sleep would set him up for several hours. Something he picked up in his ring career.

At 6 o'clock on the morning of Sunday, 25th July 1965, following a tip-off, the police found his body on the front seat, the driver's seat, of his car, which was parked in its usual place behind his restaurant. A rifle was in his mouth. His head was blown off. He was 46. At the inquest the coroner returned a verdict of suicide. This despite the fact that the rifle which did the damage was so long that his fingers, his hands, were still eight inches short of reaching the trigger. There was also the other major fact that within a few hours of the coroner's verdict all papers, files, notes and other evidence went missing from the records of New Scotland Yard. And remain so to this day.

Freddie Mills was a very courageous man – he proved that during his 14 years in the professional ring. He spoke his mind, he was honest, and he loved life. In May of that year he sat in his restaurant telling me of his plans and ambitions for the future for his wife and two kiddies.

No way did Freddie Mills commit suicide.

The greatest example I have seen of the magic and correct use of ballyhoo was demonstrated by Cassius Clay – Muhammad Ali. It was May 1963. Clay, as he was then, had signed to meet our own British Heavyweight Champion, Henry Cooper, over ten rounds in June at Wembley Stadium. Clay had arrived on these shores some three weeks before the fight. Publicity for the former Olympic Games Light Heavyweight Champion had preceded him. A few verses of poetry, insulting his opponent, always made good copy, and, though this was only his 19th fight, he'd won them all, 14 by a knockout. But Archie Moore had been the only class fighter he had met and beaten, until he stepped into the ring with 'Our Enry' on 18th June. We had arranged, through Harry Levene, to have Cassius live in our *Sportsview* studio that particular Wednesday evening. David Coleman was interviewing him, and Cassius, with his entourage of six or seven, arrived in Studio D at 8.30 p.m. sharp, 45 minutes before we went on the air.

Rehearsal with Cassius was unnecessary so, whilst the cameras and sound were being lined up for transmission, the three of us, Cassius, David and I, sat in the studio chatting about the interview, which I had scheduled to last for five minutes. The usual points were discussed. How was training going, hopes for the future, etc. Cassius was chatting about his fight six months earlier with Archie Moore:

Cassius: So in the third round I'm moving and talking. He's stepping on my feet, swearing at me. Hitting me on the back of my neck. Boy, I learnt so many tricks from Archie that night.

David Coleman: Sounds more like the Chicago race riots to me!

Cassius: (Smiling) You mention that, boy, and I'll get up and walk out.

Silence.
A long silence.
We looked at each other in turn. I banged the coffee table with my hand. David snapped his fingers and Cassius started to nod his head, quietly saying, 'That's it. That's it. I will make you all famous.' So we planned for the interview to take a certain format, and after $4\frac{1}{2}$ minutes, with 30 seconds left, I got a signal to David and he brought in the question of Cassius's fight with Archie Moore. At 9.45 that late May evening, this exploded onto the screens:

David Coleman: So what you really mean, Cassius, is that fighting Archie Moore was more like being involved in the Chicago race riots.

Cassius: What do you mean, what I really mean. I know what I meant and no way whatsoever did I imply anything like that. I take that remark as a big insult, and I didn't come here to be insulted, and I am not going to sit here and be insulted.

And so saying, he jumped up, stepped off the slightly raised interview rostrum and strode towards the studio door, quickly followed by his entourage, who had been sitting quite smugly out of camera shot. This act of Clay's was just as big a surprise to them as it was to 9½ million viewers. Cass was yelling his head off about 'insulting remarks' and 'I'll teach you all on 18th June.'

Into the lift he strode, and he bellowed to a bewildered lift attendant to take him to the ground floor, during which journey he still raged on about being insulted. Up and down the entrance hall of Lime Grove strode this huge athlete, bitterly complaining about his treatment. Then one of his handlers appeared with the car and off they shot up Lime Grove with car doors still being slammed, on their way back to the Savoy Hotel. Within minutes the press boys were arriving. They spoke to the still-quivering commissionaire who had been on duty in the reception hall, and to the lift attendant, both of whom corroborated the story of an irate Cassius Clay complaining bitterly of his treatment by the BBC sports department and of being personally insulted.

By ten past ten we were off the air and were ensconced in one of the hospitality rooms just by the entrance of Lime Grove. Peter Dimmock, by now fully in on our secret, had made a tactful statement to the dozen or so pressmen gathered in the entrance hall: Cassius Clay had obviously misinterpreted our question – no insult was intended.

At about 10.30 the telephone in our hospitality room rang. I picked it up. 'Hello, Sportsview, Alec Weeks speaking.'

Back came a deep, smooth chuckle. 'Told you I'd make you famous, boy. You stick with Cassius Clay and you'll get right to the top. See you at Wembley on 18th June.'

The line went dead. Cass had continued complaining in the foyer of the Savoy and then disappeared into his room, refusing to make any further comment or to see or speak to the press. The following morning every newspaper carried comment on the *Sportsview* interview, most on the front page.

The BBC got publicity, Clay got publicity, and thousands of additional tickets for the fight were sold the following day. *Sportsview* had certainly lived up to its motto: 'Tomorrow's headlines, tonight'. I did not see Clay on the 18th, not in person. I was at the fight, which we televised live, and it must have been the nearest Clay had been to a defeat in his two and a half years of professional boxing.

Cooper took the first two rounds, and flattened Clay at the end of the fourth with one of the neatest left hooks ever thrown in a British ring. Halfway through the intermission Clay's glove suddenly burst, and the one-minute interval lasted five seconds under two minutes. That was enough time for Clay to recover his scrambled senses. Out he came for the fifth, worked on Cooper's left eye, and the fight was stopped in favour of the American. A near squeak for Clay, but what a showman. Eight months later he won the World Heavyweight title.

Over the next twenty years or so I would often see Cassius, or Muhammad Ali, as he became known. It would be at some large function or other, a dinner, a fight promotion, some publicity stunt, lots of different places. He would always recognise me, give me a shake of the hand, or a wave if in the distance. In 1980 at the Essex Hotel, New York, I stepped into the elevator to take me to my floor. Just before the door closed, in stepped Muhammad. He nodded. I said, 'I've just finished reading your book, *The Greatest*. It was good, very good.'

'Naturally,' said Ali. 'How are all my friends at the BBC?' The elevator had reached his floor. 'Remember me to Mr David [Coleman].' And so saying, this great lithe athlete stepped out of the lift. He fought Larry Holmes in October that year. Way past his best, he took the biggest beating of his life and retired from the ring after that – he had to.

Four years later, during the Los Angeles Olympics, I was in my office within the international broadcasting centre when I was aware of a little figure standing on the other side of my desk. I looked up. There was a little greasy-looking man, about 40. He leant forward. 'How would you like an interview with the great Muhammad Ali? You can have him for 200 dollars cash. He's just outside.'

I didn't reply, but got up and went to the office door. Standing there was this huge bulk of a man. His hands were shaking, so also was his head. I spoke to him. 'Hi, Muhammad, it's me, Alec Weeks, from the BBC in London.' The spaceless, flat eyes didn't blink. He just stood and looked at the direction the voice came from. Did a look of recognition flash over that face? I like to think so.

I shoved a fistful of dollars into his jacket pocket, whereupon the greasy little man took the great Muhammad's hand and led him down the corridor to some other broadcasting organisation. Ali's

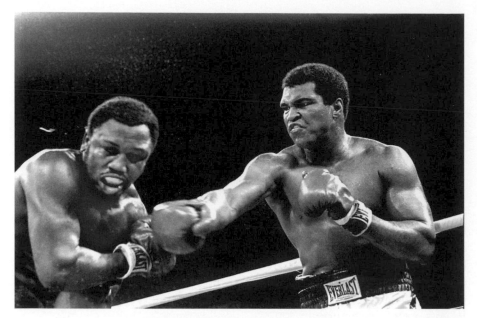

Muhammed Ali, 'The Greatest'. © EMPICS

feet shuffled along, his great frame twitching and shaking. As this shell of a man disappeared from sight, in my mind I was remembering the great athlete of the '60s and '70s. The fastest heavyweight of all time. 'Float like a butterfly, sting like a bee.' He was good. So very, very good.

Chapter Five

DOA *(family viewing)*

It started, like all these things, in a fairly quiet manner. The week before Christmas 1962 there were heavy frosts, frosts that remained bitter until Christmas Eve – remember them? – and then on Christmas morning the heavens parted. It snowed and snowed and snowed. For four days, it snowed. By 2 p.m. on Christmas Day I had dragged Controller Stuart Hood away from his Christmas lunch to explain to him the problems of filling a 5-hour *Grandstand* transmission the following day, and to ask his permission to fill an hour and a half of that with a feature film. He agreed. So on Boxing Day we planned for sport from 12.30 to 15.00, then a feature film, and finally sports results from 16.45 until 17.30. But by 12.25, five minutes before transmission, only three boxers had arrived at Nottingham; one motorcyclist at a remote farm in Leicestershire for moto-cross; and one snooker player in another studio in Lime Grove, the evergreen Joe Davis. Editor Ronnie Noble spoke to him on the phone, explained the situation and finished by saying, 'So, Joe, we'll cut to you about 12.35. Pad out, do something, until the boxers and motorcyclists arrive.'

So for five minutes at 12.30 David Coleman became a Met Office expert on the disasters of the weather for British sport and then over to the master, Joe Davis. All alone, as his opponent was also a victim of the weather, he proceeded to put on an exhibition of trick shots the like of which I had never seen before or since. It was snooker magic. He made the coloured balls do seemingly impossible things. Not a word was spoken. No commentary, just the sound of snooker ball hitting snooker ball. For 58 minutes he performed, unhurried and with effortless perfection, and then four boxers of matching height arrived and we went to amateur boxing at Nottingham, where people were brought in out of the snow-covered streets, given a cup of hot coffee and ushered into ringside seats to provide a spectator background!

At 2 p.m., ten motorcyclists got underway for what was to be a new sport on television: moto-cross. Because the competitors revelled in these conditions we had moto-cross on the screen from that Saturday until the end of the freeze in early March. For their cooperation we gave them a four-year contract, and by 1968 we had so oversaturated the screen with moto-cross, we virtually killed the sport as a television spectacle through overexposure.

But let me stay with that Boxing Day *Grandstand* of 1962. The feature film which had been hurriedly found by a member of the planning department was a minor Hollywood A-movie entitled *Dead on Arrival*, starring Edmund O'Brien. Neither Ronnie nor I had seen or heard anything about the film, but it was obviously a whodunnit that would surely keep our viewers happy for a couple of hours. The film was the easy bit.

It hit the screen with a bang at 3 p.m. exactly. Up in the control-room gallery we relaxed. The marvellous secretaries, who were always a tower of strength during problem times, produced some succulent sandwiches and lovely sweet coffee (surely laced with something, because within a few minutes, one was in a warm, relaxed glow).

The first screen murder hit the viewer at 3.10 p.m. The second by 3.15. By 3.30, five were dead. Hundreds of mothers were making indignant and horrified requests to the Television Centre exchange for the film to be faded at once. As it was such a cold day most people, especially the kids, were indoors watching television, and here we were showing a film for family viewing on how to murder dozens of people. Now that in itself was worrying, but the premeditated method of slaughter was presented in all its simplicity that Saturday afternoon to thousands of kids: breaking a thermometer and placing a drop of mercury into the victim's food.

It looked so easy and it horrified the mums and dads. Eleven times! The TV Centre PBX did a marvellous job of fending off irate viewers, but some got through: 'Twenty minutes ago my twin 12-year-olds disappeared. I went looking for them. I can't find them, but both thermometers have disappeared. What are you going to do about it?' 'Is this what is called family viewing? Take it off immediately!' 'How dare you put this film on. I'm the mother of

74

five children who have been glued to the screen ever since this film started. You can have no idea what five children are capable of.'

The following week we chose something simple. *High Noon.*

Author directing *Grandstand* in 1962 from Lime Grove Studios.

Chapter Six

Offside

The first soccer match I ever directed for television was in 1959, the second half of a European Cup quarter-final between Burnley and Hamburg. In those days Burnley had a great team containing Jimmy McIlroy, Ray Pointer and Jimmy Adamson, to name just a few. The match was live and the fee the BBC paid was £250. I think the corporation is required to pay slightly more nowadays!

When one thinks of soccer on the screen only one programme comes to mind: *Match of the Day*, the *Match of the Day* of the '60s and '70s. Its first transmission was on 22nd August 1964. The match was Liverpool v. Arsenal. I worked as the producer in the videotape area on the first six programmes.

To put soccer on the screen was nothing new, but to cover a match live from the ground, record on videotape and transmit the edited cut-down version within a few hours of the event was unheard of. Joe Public had been weaned on badly shot, poorly edited, bad-quality film, mainly because it had been shot and processed in record time, whereas film needed to be treated with respect and leisurely, loving care.

Videotape was different. Within minutes, seconds, we could transmit; one could also record again and again on the same piece of tape; it was robust, it was cheap, and its comparison with live transmission was excellent. By August 1964 six machines stood proudly in the basement of Television Centre.

So, at 2.45 p.m. on Saturday, 22nd August 1964 a videotape machine recorded the introduction and first half of Liverpool v. Arsenal (commentator Kenneth Wolstenholme, director Alan Chivers) until 3.45 p.m., when another machine took over for the second half whilst editing began on the first. I use the word 'editing'.

77

'Butchering' would be more appropriate. We were due on the air at 6.30 p.m. for this first *Match of the Day*. The match finished at 4.50 p.m. The time available to edit 90 minutes down to a 45-minute transmission was, to say the least, in short supply; and, as we had only edited six matches on videotape prior to this one, experience was another commodity we needed. Liverpool had a pretty active number five playing that day, Ron Yeats. We found an 'out' point on a piece of activity in the first half – a throw-in taken by Ron Yeats. Just as the ball left his big hands, snip went the scissors and we spooled off the next ten minutes of play and picked up with the ball in midfield. A bit of glue, a bit of tape and off we spooled, looking for another editing point.

On transmission, when that particular edit came up not only was it a world-record throw-in, the ball being thrown by Ron Yeats from the near side to the far side, but it also landed at the feet of ... Ron Yeats! The match, or the television version, was full of interesting touches like that.

The second week saw us on the air 30 minutes later, 7 p.m.; the third and fourth weeks at 7.30 p.m.; then after that it was never before 10 p.m.

It was all very well for the then Head of Sport, Bryan Cowgill, to wave a contract in the air signed by the Secretary of the Football League, Alan Hardacre. Great achievement that it was, the game still had to be put on to the screen.

One of the reasons why England was awarded the 1966 World Cup was the guarantee that all matches would be covered with electronic cameras. Sure, we had transmitted football on BBC, but mainly on film. Hence *Match of the Day*. Even so, this was on BBC2, and transmitted in the London area only, though by the end of the year viewers in the Midlands could also see it. But from August '64 until July '66 we had 23 months to train hand-picked cameramen and engineers, who were more used to covering an opera one day and a dog show the next. Though the gentlemen of the Football League had approved the idea and the contract in general, the club directors were a different story. To some we were a cross between the tax collector and a heavy dose of flu. Their attitude was, 'You are only an overnight wonder, here today and gone tomorrow', or 'No way could you place your cameras in the stands, taking up spectator space'. We always aimed for two of our main cameras to have clear visibility of the pitch, the other two to be low down, as close to the touchline as one could get. So, generally, the best place was either at the rear of the stand or on a camera platform fixed to the girders of the roof.

Now, some of these stands had been built in the late 1890s and certainly very few of them had received a touch of paint. We had problems on many an occasion. In early 1965, by now transmitting to viewers in the Midland region, we visited Leicester City. We received warm greetings and cooperation from the Club Secretary, Eddie Plumley; unlike their directors, most club secretaries and groundsmen were helpful. We finally decided to build a rostrum in the roof, suspending it from the girders rather like a modern-day dormer window. With two cameras and directional microphones would be a couple of cameramen, two sound staff, the commentator, Ken Wolstenholme, and a stage manager. Everyone would be up and on the platform by 2.30 – the ladder would be pulled up after the last climber to avoid obstructing the spectators underneath – and remaining up on that platform until 4.45. (Yes, I know what your next question is. Someone would have taken up with them an empty bucket for use in emergencies only, i.e. if someone was caught short.) This match was in March and the weather had been dry for some time, certainly since the building of this rostrum in the roof. However, soon after the kick-off the weather changed and it started to rain, heavily, and to pour through little gaps in the roof, right on to the football directors, who were sitting immediately under the television rostrum. Club Secretary Eddie Plumley ran around the posh directors' enclosure handing out umbrellas to the swearing VIPs. Afterwards I arranged for the gaps to be patched up and for the ownership of the rostrum to become Leicester City's; it remained so for five years until the club replaced it with a permanent steel girder job.

Gradually during that first season *Match of the Day* began to be appreciated by not only the managers but by mature players such as Tom Finney, Johnny Haynes and Bobby Charlton. 'How good are they? We play them next week. Let's watch *Match of the Day*.' Most of the club directors respected their views. It was surprising how many number 9 players wanted to know which camera to run to when they scored. The players' strip often gave one headaches. On black and white television blue and red looked very much alike, so we had to talk the superstitious visiting manager into allowing his team to play in a different strip.

Then there was the colour of the ball. Often in the mid-60s the popular shade of match ball was an orangey colour, which on black and white TV was the same colour as the spectators' faces. If the background to the ball was a sea of faces the cameramen eventually lost the ball, so one always requested the club to provide a white or bright-yellow ball. There was the occasion when our request got overlooked. One such was at Old Trafford, Manchester United v. Derby County. Out trotted the referee, Clive Thomas, carrying the match ball, which according to the Football-League rules has to remain the match ball throughout the game. It was bright orange. There was nothing we could do before kick-off, except direct all cameras to play the coverage much wider than usual, hoping to keep the ball in shot. At half-time we talked Clive into allowing us to 'look after the match ball'. We promptly put the whole thing into a carefully prepared bucket of bleach. It was a very pale ball that took the field for the second half.

It didn't take the League clubs long to latch onto the opportunities of making 'a little bit more brass'. During the winter months we would often ask for the floodlighting to be switched on from the kick-off, and, although that would cost only an extra £8 or £10, I would regularly receive from certain clubs an invoice for £50. Some clubs always knew how to make a little extra money!

Advertising was a perfect example. I think stadium advertising, especially perimeter adverts, gave me more headaches than anything else in my 30 years in OBs. At the beginning of each season football clubs would sign a contract with particular advertising firms, who in turn would inform the clubs which adverts were being displayed for the next 12 months. Some boards just displayed local shops or produce. For instance, at Maine Road, home of Manchester City, one of the many perimeter boards read 'D.B. Green, your local greengrocer' etc., and our Mr Green had paid the club one hundred pounds for a two-year contract.

Now, within every contract that the BBC had with any organisation, the following words were clearly displayed: 'This outside broadcast will not be used for the purpose of advertising'. Now, this was included in the BBC's contract with the Football League and within the facilities letter that I gave the club about two weeks before the broadcast of the match. Of course, the gentlemen of the advertising world were and are very astute, and it did not take them long to grasp the opportunity of making some profit for themselves and for the clubs. Big profit!

For the remainder of 1964 *Match of the Day* was transmitted exclusively on BBC2, which reached the London area only. In January '65 it was transmitting up to the Midland region. It was from that time onwards, especially when broadcasting from the grounds for the second or third time, that we, I, became aware of different adverts on certain perimeter hoardings, especially the ones behind the goals and by the halfway line. At first it was just the one board that was changed, but the problem just grew and grew. The clubs were receiving a very nice sum of money when matches were televised. The BBC had a very good contract, and nothing, no one, would be allowed to rock that boat.

1964. *Match of the Day*. Note the old-fashioned fixed lens.

© BBC

I made sure a list of all adverts (what and where they were) was kept, but the advertisers pulled all the tricks. The size and heights of the perimeter boards gradually increased. They began to get closer to the touchline, and on the far side another row of boards was frequently erected behind the original row. I began to get the riggers of the crew, the lads who fixed all the cable around the stadium, to remove the really objectionable adverts five minutes

81

before the match. Sometimes a little force was necessary, but bruised knuckles never harmed anyone and besides our lads always appreciated a tip from me.

As far as I was concerned it was only a matter of time before the problem blew up in our faces. It did in March 1966 at Villa Park on the occasion of the FA Cup Semi-Final. Between 6 p.m. Friday and 9 a.m. Saturday the advertisers had transformed the ground. Every advert had been changed, every board was bigger and closer to the pitch and even the wording and print was larger. I spent hours arguing with officials of the club, of the FA, even the advertisers. Finally I phoned Peter Dimmock at his home in West London. It was now 1.30 p.m. I explained everything to him and told him I favoured pulling out. He asked a few questions then, realising I was quite serious about pulling out, said, 'I'll phone back within half an hour.' It was 2.15 p.m. when he finally rang. He'd been on to the FA, the Football League, the BBC's solicitor, and, in short, a meeting with all concerned, including the advertisers, was convened for the following Tuesday. He finished with, 'Now, Weeksy, cover the match and try not seeing any of the adverts around the pitch. Miss them.' I took the cameramen into my confidence but knew that it was an impossible task for them and for me. The advertisers had a field day. They must have made a packet.

At the meeting, which went on for several hours, a general agreement was reached. The clubs had to give us, the BBC, seven days' notice and details of the advertising. It solved nothing. In other words they were using the broadcast for the purpose of advertising.

Another source where fortunes were made through televised football, and I really mean fortunes, was floodlighting. In early '68 it had been decided that in the autumn of '69 we would be transmitting in colour on a daily basis. Stadium lighting at all Football League grounds was simply not adequate. We had to convince the First Division clubs of what was required to improve their lights. At the majority of clubs it required the installation of powerful bulbs and light sockets. Not an impossible job, not if one's stadium already had at least four tall lighting pylons. But the get-rich-quick boys were one step ahead of television. They approached the clubs and sold them an 'improved' lighting installation for between fifteen and twenty thousand pounds a time. Most of the bulbs were purchased from Morocco, were second-hand and lasted only a few months. I was approached by Chelsea FC, who were one of the clubs that had been approached. They had heard rumours of the scam, but hadn't passed over any money. We had, in our outside-broadcast department, a lighting engineer, Brian Wilkes, who was quite brilliant on the subject of floodlighting. In short, I took him along to Chelsea FC, and that was the beginning of a new life for Brian for the next three years at least, visiting and studying the floodlighting at every First Division club and some in the Second Division. He would write up a synopsis of what was required, but, and this was the important point, he would give each club an introduction to two or three professional lighting installers that the BBC recommended. The consultation and 12-page reports submitted by Brian cost the clubs nothing whatsoever. They were only requested to treat Brian's consultation in a discreet manner.

Nevertheless, nine clubs and two world-famous stadiums still parted with thousands of pounds to the cowboys. Some still live comfortably in their mansions in Derbyshire.

In those days of the mid-60s the 'scanners' (our nickname for the OB vans) were quite small. The director was sitting within an area about 8 by 6 feet. In front of him were a dozen or so small six-inch monitors, each carrying the output of the four cameras; the director, the commentator and the cameramen were all in communication with each other, each endeavouring to dovetail together. A good director will guide his cameramen, coach them, bully, shout, scream at them, even applaud and congratulate them on an exceptional shot. A good commentator knows his job is to verbally write the caption under the picture and knows when to shut up. The same principle applies to a TV director: a good one knows when not to cut.

When director, commentator and cameraman all click together, never missing a single shot, it really is exhilarating, to say the least. Better than sex!

The Januaries and Februaries of '65 and '66 brought harsh bitter winters, and often, especially for an evening match, the temperature was well below freezing. Five minutes after the final whistle the four cameramen returned to the scanner, where I had been ensconced in the warmth for a couple of hours. None could speak; one or two managed a hoarse croak, but all had a black impression around their eyes and nose where they had pressed their face hard into the rubber-edged viewfinder to keep out the cold. The exposed chin and mouth were encrusted with frost and ice; they could hardly move their frozen fingers and arms. Ipswich Town provided the solution. On any similar days they ensured each exposed operator, camera – or sound – man was supplied, at half-time and again at full-time, with a miniature bottle of brandy. That worked.

One needed a certain amount of luck during those winter months. We were rigged in at West Bromwich Albion when, at 8 a.m. on the day of the game the referee, after walking around the pitch, declared that the match was off. I made a few phone calls, to the Met Office in TV Centre, to the Football League, and finally to my old friend, Eddie Plumley of Leicester City who that day were playing Burnley. By 11 a.m. we had de-rigged all equipment and set off for Leicester. Many roads were closed and the icy conditions had to be taken carefully. We covered the 35 miles in just under 2 hours. Eddie made sure the right doors and gates were open and the cables and cameras started to be put into position. In the '60s it took four men to lift and carry the heavy cameras to the rear of the stand; coaxial camera cable was as thick as one's wrist – two inches. At Leicester City, to rig and equip four cameras required about 400–500 feet per camera; then the microphone cables for commentary and effects. Time was ticking by. We had arrived just after 1 p.m. and by 1.30, when the turnstiles for Joe Public were opened, we had just about found power and plugged up the four large vehicles. By 2.30 we had distributed all the equipment. It still had to be plugged up and tested, and in the '60s this equipment always took some time to test. Eddie Plumley and his staff were going around to our 21 crew with mugs of steaming soup. At 2.55 the players came onto the pitch; at 3, kick-off. We needed to show patience, as one by one the cameras were switched on and found to be working; then they had to be 'matched': all the greys, whites, blacks on all cameras had to be the same. Half-time came. The score was still nil-nil. Everything worked. We began passing the pictures to switching transmitters at a place just outside Coventry. It had taken two and a half hours to do what normally took four hours. The players came back onto the pitch. Sound and vision were now being received at TV Centre, London. Cue Barry Davies. This is where Lady Luck stepped in. It was nil-nil at kick-off for the second half, but seven goals were scored in the match, which was won by Leicester 4–3. Not a goal was missed. Now, that was a match I remember.

But life is not kind all the time. The winter of the following year, the same thing occurred. We did it once. We would, of course, do the same thing again. This time we even had everything working by the kick-off. BUT. The radio-links vehicle, positioned at Coventry, couldn't get up a hill to receive our pictures being transmitted from the ground. The road was too icy and this very important link was necessary to enable the pictures and sound to be passed through to London. We had to show videotape highlights of the season in that evening's *Match of the Day*. Our Head of Sport, Bryan Cowgill, ranted and screamed down the phone to me in the scanner, and again when I returned to TV Centre. And again when I sat in my office after transmission. Even when I arrived home at Byfleet. He was like that. Often.

But to return to the 'Good Guys', normally a good cameraman can make a boring match exciting – cameramen of the likes of Tony Wigley, Barry Chaston, Keith Williams, Pete Hill and Trevor Wimlett. But if I had to select one, and one only, I would plump for Phil Wilson of the Midlands region. He was fast, artistic and knew his football better than many of today's so-called pundits. If Phil had a special dramatic shot he would shout over his talkback, 'three, three, three, three.' Over the years I came to rely on his brilliance, and knew what a gigantic shot he would produce of some incident on the pitch. Without even looking at his preview monitor I would transmit his shot.

I directed matches on *Match of the Day* from 1965 until 1987 and was its executive producer from 1965 until 1980, but the period that gave me my biggest headaches, and also my greatest satisfaction, was those six years between 1964 and 1970.

So we were very much a team whenever we arrived at an outside broadcast, whether that was athletics, boxing, racing or football. We shared everything, not just the broadcast but the hardships, and the expenses. We were all on the same expenses allowance, so if, say, ten of us had dinner together we would automatically split the bill ten ways. It was a custom that had grown up with the Beeb and it was fair to everyone. Or not quite everyone.

It nicely finished off a long day's work on a Saturday to travel back on the 6.30 p.m. from Manchester or Liverpool in the Pullman dining car. There was normally a group of five or six of us. A well-cooked three-course meal accompanied by a bottle of Bordeaux, followed by a nice cigar, and one forgot the problems of the day. But I will never forget the sight of this famous personality moving

85

up and down the now-empty dining car, collecting the screwed-up receipts, muttering, 'These will help me with my tax return.' Also, having paid one's share of the restaurant bill, one naturally left a 10 per cent tip – let's say it was a pound. Our personality would often be the last to leave the table, and I realised why later, when returning for some cigarettes I had left: there was our personality collecting up the tips we had all left. 'My need is greater than a waiter's.' I saw this act repeated on several occasions.

Then there was another gentleman who thought he could get away with the Crown jewels. It was 1980, Moscow. By now I was in charge of major sporting events, which included the Moscow Olympics. Now, it was a well-known fact that sterling or dollar hard currency would fetch double the official exchange rate. So, our 'spiv' decided to stand on the corner of Red Square, asking the passing Muscovites, 'Anyone want some dollars?', and waving a fistful of the American currency in the air. He kept this up for about half an hour until he saw in the distance an approaching policeman. It didn't occur to him that not all the Moscow Police wore uniforms; some wore plain clothes. It was about 7 p.m. I was in the BBC's office in the Olympic broadcasting centre. The phone rings. A guttural Russian-sounding English-speaking voice asks to speak to me. I identify myself. 'Mr Weeks, Colonel—— of the KGB. Your Mr—— was seen and heard between 6 and 6.30 p.m. to be standing on the corner of Red Square and attempting to sell hard American currency – dollars. This, Mr Weeks, is against all USSR principles, and if your Mr—— repeats this he will be removed immediately.' He rang off. Whether 'remove immediately' represented assassination or just the next plane to London, I know not. I told our spiv to report at once to the office, where I took him into a corner and gave him a jolly good bollocking.

I can also think of another occasion when 'truth will out'. There were about a dozen boys and girls from the department at the club bar, which included one famous presenter at the rear, supping up all the drinks that everyone was buying him. Suddenly the gang disappeared, leaving just myself and our personality, who had yet to buy a round, a fact I took the opportunity of pointing out to him. 'Why should I, Alec? Tonight, when you go home and sit down for dinner with your wife and children, you can tell them that today you had the honour of buying me a drink.' Cannot print my reply, but it only takes one or two rotten apples...

By the early 1970s seven or eight matches were covered each Saturday by the two networks. Fifteen to twenty minutes after the final whistle managers, and sometimes players, were being interviewed. They would be contracted a few days later, details of which were eventually passed to the Inland Revenue who took a large share of the fee. By the mid-70s all were asking to be paid in cash, on the spot or 'in kind'. That brought forth some amusing requests: Joe Mercer, Jock Stein and Dave Sexton asked for bouquets of flowers to be sent to their wives; Brian Clough, 'A bottle of Champagne, young man'. Which, if he had to travel to the studio, became 'a crate'. Poultry was a popular request around Christmas. So also was a reservation for two in a local fashionable restaurant. It was always roughly what they would have been contracted for. Bill Shankly gave me a shock. It was April 1974. The Cup Final was just a few weeks away. Liverpool versus Newcastle. I was in Bill's office, a fistful of contracts in my hands for us to interview Bill during the week of and on the day of the Final. Seven in all totalling £450. Bill was scratching his signature on the different contracts when he suddenly stopped. He slammed the pen down, grabbed all the contracts in his hands, tore the lot into different pieces, shouting, 'No. No. No.'

As the pieces were fluttering down, my brain was working overtime. 'I mustn't leave here without his signature. How much higher can I go?'

Bill took two steps in my direction, grasped me by my lapels and snarled in that Scottish way, 'How much have ye git on yer?' My hand flashed to my back pocket – one always obeyed Bill Shankly. 'Thirty-five pounds, Bill.'

'Give it to me, Alick.'

I fished out the notes. He snatched them out of my hand saying, 'Why should I pay the Inland Revenue for all those interviews?' We shook hands and the BBC got all their interviews that year with Bill Shankly for £35.

That act compares with the famous personality we wanted as our expert summariser at the World Cup, FA Cup and European Cup Final. Ten major soccer events in all. We agreed terms. Contracts were sent out. Publicity Department notified the nationals. All seemed agreed. Our personality popped in to see us. Sam Leitch, the football editor at that time, called me over to his office. All very friendly until our personality said, 'I want very little under contract. I want cash, most in expenses. International air tickets, hotel bookings, all for my wife and me.'

He didn't work for us for a long long time. What was I saying about rotten apples?

The Charity Shield, August 1968, Manchester United against Tottenham Hotspur, played at Old Trafford. This would be our first soccer match in colour. Wimbledon in June had taken the television honours, but I was determined that *Match of the Day* would not be very far behind, even though only viewers who received BBC2 and had a colour receiver could see it. If it was a good match the publicity for the Beeb would be enormous. I organised a large suite in the Midland Hotel, invitations to all the northern press, plenty of drinks and three very large rented colour-television sets. Mrs Louis Edwards, wife of the Manchester United Chairman, was quite a Manchester trendsetter. She had also organised a party at her palatial house, and anyone who was anyone in Manchester society was invited: the Lord Mayor, the Chief Constable, the local beauty queen – you name it, they were there, not only to eat and drink the best, but to see Manchester United in glorious colour on the screen for the first time. And what a match! Even the Spurs goalkeeper, Pat Jennings, scored with a goal kick, and by half-time the score was two each. We all relaxed at half-time, content with the knowledge that this first half would look sensational on the box that night.

Now, the furthest we had ever recorded in colour was the distance from Wimbledon to Television Centre at Shepherd's Bush, and, in those days of colour, we learnt as we went along. From Old Trafford to Television Centre videotape machines was only 198 miles, and colour reception in London was excellent. Just before the second half started, I got a call from the *Match of the Day* programme assistant in London, Roy Norton (who, week in, week out, methodically logged all the games' highlights). 'Stupid thing, Alec, nothing to worry about, but just spotted (played back) a few minutes of the first half, and this bloody machine can only play back in black and white. Anyway, nothing to worry about, will put it on one of the spare machines whilst the second half is on. Hope this half is as good as the first.'

It was even better. But this slight problem nagged away in my head until the final whistle. The phone rang. 'Look, chum, didn't want to worry you whilst you were directing the match, but I've had the top engineers on duty here playing back the first half and for some unknown reason it cannot be recorded in colour. We can see it in colour, but cannot record it. So tonight's transmission has got to be, as usual, in black in white.' I was struck dumb. We still had a programme, but what about the Manchester press reception? Ron Crowther of the *Daily Mail* and Dennis Lowe of the *Telegraph* were heroes. I explained to them what had happened and they personally contacted 60 members of the press and stood them all down. Only Frank McGhee of the *Daily Mirror* got nasty on the Monday: 'BBC PUT THE WRONG TYPE OF FILM IN THEIR CAMERAS'. How ignorance is bliss! But, I took it upon myself to explain fully to Manchester United Secretary Leslie Olive and Manager Matt Busby, and by 5.45 p.m. I felt I had retrieved at least a little from a disastrous incident.

Then: 'The Chairman would like to see you, Alec,' says Leslie Olive, leading me into the directors' boardroom. All of them were there, partaking of a drink or two.

'Ah, Alec,' says Louis Edwards, 'I don't think you have met my wife.' He led me to a corner where the elegantly dressed Mrs Edwards stood. Everyone disappeared, and suddenly I was alone with the formidable Mrs Edwards, who proceeded verbally to tear strips off me: '...the biggest reception of the year ruined ... personally send the BBC the bill ... will never watch the BBC again ... will ban you and your cameras from Old Trafford for life.' And so the barrage went on until she stamped off.

I was still shaking when a hand rested lightly on my shoulder, and there was Matt Busby's broad Scottish tone clearing my head. 'Here, laddie, get this brandy inside you. You need it more than I do.'

It was no secret that in the 60s competition between the sports departments of the BBC and ITV was fierce to say the least. But all the bickering, fighting and knocking in public came to a head at the Cup Final in 1969, between Manchester City and Leicester City.

It started with an innocuous remark by Joe Mercer, the manager of Manchester City. It might have been a fairly harmless comment about the Wembley pitch by 'Uncle Joe', but it was to get an earth-shattering reaction from the ever-hungry media, written and electronic. Way back in September of the previous year, the Horse of the Year Show was staged, for the first time, at Wembley Stadium. Showjumping in the '60s was playing to packed houses, and at least two hours of events were transmitted live every day. During the week of daily jumping events it rained and rained. The public were under cover, and it was only the riders and horses that got wet, however not only was the hallowed stadium turf churned up, with ton after ton of horseflesh thumping into the ground, it was not long before the ground staff began to realise that the drainage under the pitch had been very badly damaged.

The normally wonderfully drained pitch, scene of hundreds of famous world-shattering events, was now in a very sorry state. It was a wet winter and an even wetter spring. The water seemed to just float on the grass. The Wembley ground staff worked overtime – forking, aerating – but all to no avail. Come May and the eve of the Cup Final (the Friday afternoon, to be exact, when the teams take a stroll around the pitch 24 hours before the kick-off), I'm walking alongside Uncle Joe when, after taking a dozen steps, he yelled, 'It's a cabbage patch! I've seen better at the council allotments in Moss Side [Manchester].' The press, the reporters, the members of the media, froze, then dived on Joe, firing hundreds of questions at him. I stepped out. All I wanted was a good match the following day with, if possible, plenty of goals. If Uncle Joe's cabbage patch could provide a slip at the wrong time and a hatful of goals, then I was a happy man.

This little incident was to set the scene of what turned out, for me, to be a very unusual Cup Final.

Tony Flanagan was the producer for ITV. I was the Beeb's. George Stanton, the general manager of Wembley Stadium, called both of us together a week before the match and told us he was 'cleaning up the pitch for the lap of honour'. This meant no interviews on the pitch, only down the mouth of the tunnel when the players reached there, and Wembley security passes issued to everyone.

We had outbid ITV in an exclusive contract with Manchester City worth £1,850 for interviews after the match, but we shared a non-exclusive contract with the Leicester City players for £750 each. The match was a dour, boring affair, with Manchester City winning by the odd goal over Leicester. The best team on the pitch that day were the massed bands of the Brigade of Guards at half-time. But the entertainment at ten past five on that dull Saturday afternoon had only just begun. Jimmy Dumighan, one of BBC's legmen for the day, later to be the network editor of BBC TV in Birmingham, ran alongside Colin Bell of Manchester City. His intention was to stay with him until they reached the tunnel and then guide him to the BBC cameras, and the interviews. Suddenly, on the edge of that famous pitch, which had been the scene of some crunching tackles only minutes earlier, up ran a six-footer who Jimmy thought was a trainer, as he was dressed in the FA Cup Final tracksuit of Manchester City. Crunch went his left fist, straight into Jimmy's face, breaking a back tooth as Jim staggered six feet to sit on his bottom. A cameraman shouted what was going on to me over talkback. Almost at once we saw on our own cameras Peter Lorenzo from ITV running with and interviewing the winning team. We had been double-crossed.

We could have stepped back and let ITV receive a stern rap on the knuckles from Wembley. But at the same time they had scooped us. 'Move in,' I instructed to all listening. 'Stop those bastards. Use any means possible.' With that, 15 BBC men, legmen, riggers, cameramen, tripped: 'Oh, sorry mate, I stumbled', dug in elbows: 'Oops, you OK, chum?'; even placed a hand over a stick mic: 'Now interview him, you bastards.' Tempers flared, fists flew. Players stepped over the splayed bodies of television employees. Until we got into the players' tunnel. Then the hard-bunched knuckles really started landing. Players were forgotten as heads were thumped against the tunnel wall. Knees thumped into spines. Elbows jabbed viciously into stomachs. One BBC sports executive used his folded umbrella in great style. It was a hell of a fight, involving about 40 men. There were more punches thrown than in any Harry Levene fight promotion.

It lasted 10 minutes, during which time the players, forgotten by now, by ducking and weaving had made their way to their dressing rooms, uninterviewed. Ken Jones of the *Daily Mirror*, an occasional interviewer on *Grandstand*, came striding down the tunnel to obtain quotes from the finalists for his and other newspapers. Up stood a harassed, by now extremely scruffy-looking ITV employee asking, 'Are you Ken Jones of the *Daily Mirror*?'

'I am,' replied a slightly startled Ken.

'Don't you work for *Grandstand*? snarled our ITV colleague.

'Yes,' said Ken, and in a flash a right hand to the chin had sent him flying into the dust of that Cup Final afternoon of 1969.

So on the Monday morning the front pages of all the national dailies screamed: 'BBC v. ITV PUNCH-UP ON WEMBLEY PITCH. TV CREWS CLASH AFTER CUP FINAL.'

Bryan Cowgill, Head of BBC Sport, said, 'We had an exclusive contract to interview the Manchester City players, which was known to all concerned, including ITV, who were beaten by the BBC in competition for these rights. Saturday's episode represents nothing more than a rather undignified attempt to break the contract which had been genuinely given to the BBC in preference to ITV.' End of quote.

Jimmy Hill, Head of Sport, London Weekend, said, 'We have our own contract with Manchester City players, which obviously the BBC were unaware of. It was a non-exclusive contract, but the BBC always wants to buy the rights to everything. Their way of competition is to try to destroy the opposition from even getting a chance to compete. The BBC had as many as 20 people there. Some of them were physically interfering with and manhandling our operators – pulling out plugs and trying to grab players away from us. At no time did we do anything to stop their men working. It was the BBC who were under a misapprehension, and we have breached no contract.' End of quote.

So we had an exclusive contract which really was not worth the paper it was written on. Who does one sue for breach of contract, the winners of the FA Cup Final?

There was a funny happening amidst all this disgraceful fisticuffs. Turn your memory back a few pages. While the punch-up was at its peak down in the players' tunnel – which the viewer on both channels was completely oblivious to – another one of my legmen, Bill Platts (who always worked for me at Wembley), was to stay close to the winning captain, Colin Bell of Manchester City, and take him to the TV interview room, just above the players' tunnel, the access to which was via a spiral staircase just off the now busy, hectic, TV battleground!

Bill arrived at the door of the interview room having weaved and dragged a startled Colin Bell through an avenue of violence and mayhem. There, quite rightly, the tall dignified figure of a Wembley security official was standing. 'Where's your pass?' says our security official. Bill quickly showed him the magic photographic identification tag hanging from his jacket. The security 'gentleman' nodded, then looked at Colin.

Bell's face, arms and shirt were heavily muddied from playing on the 'cabbage patch'; and, after 90 minutes of action and an exalted lap of honour around the pitch, sweat was running down his face, tracing watery lines through his muddy exterior. He was a proud man. Not only had Manchester City won the Cup, but there he was, waiting to go onto network television, holding the FA Cup in his arms, which, plinth and all, stood at two feet nine inches high.

Looking Colin straight in the eye our security said, 'Where's your pass?' Bill jumped in with, 'He doesn't need a pass. This is Colin Bell, Captain of Manchester City.'

'No pass, no entry.'

'This is his pass,' says Bill, tapping the side of the famous gleaming trophy. 'He can't play for 90 minutes with a pass around his neck.'

'Sorry, I have my instructions from the General Manager, Mr George Stanton. No one goes through that door without a pass.'

By this time commentator Kenneth Wolstenholme, up in his commentary box, is padding out like fury, waiting to hand over for the interview. He's got to the stage of talking about the flowers in HM Queen's hat. Sitting in the control van, I have heard all this security business, amidst and above the sound of the punch-up, the groans, the shouts, etc. 'Bill,' I yell. 'Get Colin to the interview studio. At once.'

Bill makes one last attempt with our security gentleman. 'Look, you hold the Cup whilst I take Colin upstairs to the interview room.'

The security man drew himself up to his full height and said, 'Are you attempting to bribe me, sir?'

With that Bill took off, dragging Colin and the famous FA Cup with him. Down the players' tunnel and outside. A quick turn to the right and up 40 steps to the upper level – the startled crowd automatically giving way at the sight of this famous athlete holding this equally famous trophy, which they had been cheering from a distance a few minutes ago, now thundering past them, taking two steps at a time. Across the crowded walkway sped Bill, through the door of the interview room, flinging a panting, out-of-breath Colin Bell into the arms of the interviewer, Wally Barnes!

A few days later, amongst other things, it was reported to me that the BBC bosses didn't think that Colin Bell, the winning captain, had given a very good interview after the match. No wonder. The poor fellow, an experienced player of dozens of internationals, must have thought that entering that players' tunnel, and what followed, was a hideous nightmare.

I tell you straight. It was a funny old Cup Final in 1969.

The great Bobby Charlton. The whole world knows of the ice-cool soccer brain of the invincible Bobby Charlton, the man who is never flummoxed, never put out, no matter what happens on the pitch – except for one occasion.

Manchester United had drawn the fourth-division side Exeter City in the third round of the FA Cup. Exeter playing at home on the famous West Country St James's Park ground. Now, the St James's Park ground is small and compact to say the least. Its covered stand, the Shed, was built in about 1910, very close to the playing area, and the edge of the roof overlooked the touchline. There was only one place to mount the cameras and that was to build a platform right on the edge of the roof of the Shed and stick two cameras and our commentator on this platform. The slight problem was that access to this platform could only be from the front, via a tall ladder from the pitch. So all concerned were up and on the platform a good 45 minutes before kick-off.

The capacity of St James's Park was then 17,000, though nowadays it is only 9,036. About 18,000 decided to pack into this little ground that afternoon, a lovely warm, friendly crowd who wanted to see their favourites in action: Georgie Best, Denis Law, Paddy Crerand, etc., and of course, Bobby Charlton.

Come half-time it was still a goalless score. Nil-all. The West Country lads and lassies were really getting excited, cheering their side on like they have never been cheered before. The second half started and about 10 minutes in there was a metallic bang and a shudder on the TV platform. Everyone froze, then someone on the platform, a cameraman, shouted into the mic that it was just a scaffolding coupling that had sprung off. Nothing much to worry about, but a check was necessary, even essential. The engineering manager alongside me darted out of the control van and dashed into the ground via the players' entrance.

As explained, the only way onto the TV platform was via a ladder positioned on the pitch. Our engineer quickly picked up the ladder lying alongside the touchline and put it against the platform, with its base planted a good 15 or 20 feet inside the pitch, just on the halfway line. What mattered to him was the safety of the crew. To hell with the FA Cup.

The match was in full flow. The referee glanced over at our senior engineer, who by now was clambering up the ladder and beginning to look minutely at every join on the scaffolding platform. The referee looked, glanced at his wristwatch, as if this sort of thing happened at the Exeter ground at 4.15 every Saturday, then carried on running, giving all his attention again to the game.

After an Exeter attack, Manchester United had the ball down by their goal and methodically started to bring it upfield. Just outside the penalty area it was passed to one Bobby Charlton, who started to take it up the left wing, right towards the ladder!

About six feet from the ladder he stopped and put his foot on the ball. He looked at the ladder. No answer. He looked up the ladder at the back of the engineer. No response. He looked at Paddy

'Now this chap could play football.'

Crerand to his right. No help there. He looked at the referee, who waved his arms forward in a signal to get on with the game. He looked back at the ladder with his hands on his hips for a full five seconds. Baffled, he started to jig up and down as if the ladder was a live, breathing opponent. He then dummied the ladder – kicked the ball with his left foot under the ladder and dashed around the other side to pick it up again with his right. The rest of the field, players on both sides, had all come to a standstill, most of them standing with their hands on their hips, just looking, waiting for the great brain to solve the problem. Charlton, having dummied the ladder, went hell for leather towards the Exeter goal, transferred his weight to his left foot and blasted away with his right.

Exeter nil, Manchester United one.

As he trotted back to the centre circle for the kick-off, surrounded by his teammates, hugging, kissing, shaking his hand, Bobby glanced over towards the ladder and waved as if to thank the ladder for a good pass that led to his goal. But for just five seconds the ice-cool brain of one of the world's most famous players was flummoxed, baffled, beaten by a workman's ladder.

So many good, British characters seem to be disappearing from the game. I was reminded of this at the passing of Brian Clough.

Brian Clough, David Coleman and Bobby Charlton at Wembley.

It was soon after 'Cloughy' had taken up his post as manager of Derby County. It was January, and Brian had been out looking at a player he fancied for his team. He got home quite late, but was glad to be indoors and away from the cold wind. He crept upstairs into the bedroom, changed into his pyjamas and quietly slid into bed. 'God,' said his wife, 'your feet are freezing.' There was a pause, then Brian, snuggling up to his wife, said, 'When we're in bed together, dear, I don't mind if you call me Brian.'

May 1967. Old Trafford. Manchester United's last match of a very successful season, was against Stoke City. With five minutes to go, a goalless draw seemed inevitable, though Manchester United had already clinched the league championship. Scottish international Paddy Crerand collided with a Stoke player, cleared the ball upfield, carried on arguing with his opponent and then, quite methodically, took the player's head in both hands and spat right in the middle of his face.

No one except our cameras noticed this. Following the match the champions quickly showered and dressed and immediately left for Ringway Airport and a chartered flight to Australia, where they were set for a five-week, six-match tour playing teams down under. Neither the team, Matt Busby, Chairman Louis Edwards, nor Paddy Crerand saw the edition of *Match of the Day* transmitted that evening, which included, in gigantic close-up, the 'spitting' incident. Paddy was judged in his absence by what the FA had seen on the screen, and he started the 1967/68 season with a three-match ban. He came looking for me on his return. It was obvious that but for my covering the incident, and certainly leaving it in the edited version, no one, certainly not the FA, would have been aware of anything. So Paddy held me completely responsible for his ban. We had a violent argument in a room in the Kensington Hilton – he threatened me, I threatened him. No one hit anyone and we went out and got tight together and have been friends ever since.

Match of the Day will always be linked with Liverpool FC. The first *MOTD*, as I have already mentioned, 22nd August 1964, was Liverpool v. Arsenal. The first match in colour on BBC1, in November 1969, was Liverpool v. West Ham. When one thinks of

97

Liverpool, eventually one thinks of one person, Bill Shankly, the man who, from way back in 1965, welcomed television. 'Let the country in, laddie, let the whole world see how great Liverpool is.' I have travelled a lot with Liverpool FC and with Bill, not only in this country but abroad. With Bill life was never dull. When a Newcastle hotel was having Highland dancing at a New Year's Eve party, at 2.15 a.m., Bill Shankly was balling out the manager with a voice far louder than the Highland band, and complaining, not because they had woken up his players, but because they had not played 'the Scottish reels', his favourite.

When losing 4–0 to Ajax in Amsterdam, Bill exploded, 'What can you do against a defensive side?'

It is said that Shanks was above all a motivator. He drove his men, his team, to do the impossible. Let me illustrate this point. It was February 1968. For weeks we had had very hard frosts, but the night before the match we were to cover at Anfield it rained, heavily. I was down at the stadium early. The whole pitch was covered in water, the ground being so hard underneath, it just would not soak away – not unless it was forked down to a depth of 4 to 5 inches. At 8 o'clock on the morning of the match there was only one man forking away in the middle of this gigantic pool of water: the great Bill Shankly. It was about this time that the riggers of our OB unit arrived at the ground. Bill came across and asked me if they could help fork the pitch for half an hour or so. I put this to them, delicately; remember, this was 1968, when one had to be aware of the unions and their wishes. Sure, our riggers agreed to help Bill for half an hour, knowing that it would take at least 50 men forking for 4 to 5 hours to clear the pitch of water. I then witnessed the most extraordinary thing. As they worked, forking away, Bill started talking to these half a dozen men: coaching, encouraging, driving them on and on and on, positioning himself roughly in the middle of the group so that they could hear his guttural Scottish tones. They did not stop after half an hour, or even after an hour, but went on for four long hours, clouds of steam rising from their bodies into the cold air, Shankly working alongside, shouting them on all the time. At 12 noon the referee arrived, inspected the pitch, carefully: 'Muddy in parts, but free from water. Yes, the match is on.'

Bill Shankly
'You'll never walk alone'.

Our riggers' hands, all six pairs, were in a terrible state, red-raw and bloody. Bill himself attended to 'my BBC lads', bathing and bandaging carefully each individual hand. In the evening, after the match (which Liverpool won of course), Bill came over to the OB van and personally took the BBC riggers into the directors' room and introduced them to the chairman of Liverpool, who in turn gave each one a little gratuity of five pounds and the biggest bottle of brandy I've ever seen. Bill, in the Liverpool programme, later dedicated the match to *his* BBC riggers, and after that would never hear a bad reference about the BBC in his presence. Now *that* was good public relations.

John Motson's Cup Final commentary, in 1979, was to produce interesting events. At the end of March, two months before the Wembley Final, David Coleman decided he wanted a complete break from television and left for the States, returning in July. Our Head of Sport, Alan Hart, decided he wanted John Motson to give the commentary on the Cup Final, and with five weeks before the big event I knew that the match would be Arsenal v. Manchester United. I was not worried about John's match commentary: even though he was inclined to talk too much, it was something I could control. But he had little experience in dealing with the build-up, the period between 2 p.m. and 2.45, before the teams marched on to the pitch. So I had John into the office for session after session of watching and listening to half a dozen previous finals, covering what to me was a very important period of the transmission. This is the time when one really, mentally, got hold of the viewer and put them, him or her, in the best seat in the stadium. Showing the thousands of fans singing, waving their colours, the close-ups, the military bands, the arriving royalty, the singing of 'Abide with Me', etc. All this was unscripted, all covered in an off-the-cuff manner. This was the opportunity for the cameramen to warm up, get the colourful shots, enjoy themselves by offering up shots of the crowds. And I always made sure I used every camera, giving confidence to the man operating the zoom. I spent hour after hour taking John through this sequence. During the two weeks prior to the final I made sure John came with me and the lads – the cameramen – to see the players training. We were made to feel at home, and we ended up all having lunch together. Afternoons were spent watching

100

videos of the teams in action. I even made sure John was equipped with a set of postcard-size photos of every player, as were the cameramen. Yes, we were ready for the big day.

Now, the match commentator never really gets involved in the Cup Final transmission until about 2 o'clock. On this occasion Frank Bough was the presenter of *Grandstand* from our studio high in the roof of the stadium. John arrived about 12 p.m., and Mike Pearce, John's allocated stage manager for the afternoon, whispered to me a little later that John had a parcel of 200 autographed photos. Of himself. I thought it was a strange thing to do before such a major event. With an hour to go John showed no nervousness whatsoever. After all, the BBC's audience from 2 o'clock would only build up to fifteen million that day.

I climbed into the scanner at about half past one, spoke to all cameras and then to John, once again repeating the words, 'We will play it off the cuff, cover the fans that are animated, waving, singing.' At five past two Frank Bough hands over to John Motson: '...and we welcome John Motson for his first of many Cup Finals. All yours, John.'

I held a wide-angle shot of Wembley, with its two well-known spires, and John starts. Within a few seconds the Man United fans started singing and waving their colours at one end of the stadium. I cut to this wonderful shot, an explosion of red and white. John's words were unexpected: 'Arsenal have a long historic presence in the FA Cup.' 'John,' I call over the talkback, 'we're on a shot of Man United fans.' Motson carries on with his history of Arsenal Football Club. I yell at him again: 'John, look at your monitor!' John still carries on. I scream at the stage manager, Mike Pearce, alongside John in the commentary box: What's happened to John's monitor?!' and it goes on like this for several minutes, me screaming my head off, John ignoring anything I say.

Finally, the Man United fans stop singing and waving their scarves and colours. Five seconds later, at the other end of the stadium, the Arsenal fans take up the challenge and they start chanting and waving their flags, etc. Our commentator says, 'Manchester United have an equal record in the FA Cup,' and so I repeat my request, my screams, my threats.

The VIP, The Duchess of Kent, arrives in the Royal Tunnel in the Royal limousine. I have a mobile camera in the Royal Tunnel and cut to a good clear close-up of HRH. Motson: 'The crowd are being entertained this afternoon by the massed band of the Brigade of Guards.' A minute later I cut to a shot of the military band. John Motson: 'Our Royal guest this afternoon is Her Highness The Duchess of Kent.' And so it went on. And on. And on. Finally, we coordinated the singing of 'Abide with Me' over which John, quite rightly, never uttered a word.

The teams came onto the pitch. The match started and John did a good commentary. Afterwards, when I challenged John over his commentary during the build-up, he reached into his briefcase and produced a dozen typed pages. 'I listened to what you had to say several weeks ago regarding the build-up and decided to write my commentary. I'm sorry if your pictures didn't match what I had written.'

Silly me!

John Motson at Wembley Stadium with stage manager Harry Coventry.

Bob Paisley will also always be Liverpool. I first knew him as trainer, then coach, then assistant manager, then manager from 1974. In his first year as manager, with Liverpool lying third in the league, he signed up a player who was Jewish. Later that day he got a phone call from a Manchester Jewish newspaper. 'Do you realise, Mr Paisley, if your player is a practising Jew he cannot play on Saturday?' 'Don't worry about that,' replied Bob, 'I already have eleven players who can't do that.'

May 1977, with Paisley arriving in Rome the day before Liverpool played Moenchengladbach in the final of the European Cup, the Italian press asked him, 'Your first visit to Rome, Signor Pastry?' 'No, I have been here before,' said Bob. 'Where? How? When? With whom?' clamoured our Italian colleagues. 'In 1945,' said Bob. 'We had a gun emplacement right in the corner of this airport.' I loved him for that remark.

It was a tragedy that the man who will always be associated with television soccer left the BBC when he was at his peak. Ken Wolstenholme had been working for the BBC since 1948, first in Manchester for radio and TV, then from the early '50s exclusively on TV.

A former RAF pilot, a DFC and a member of a Pathfinder squadron, he brought his wartime attributes into soccer. Doors would open to him; boardrooms were proud to entertain him after a match. He was a good team man, and he respected the professionalism of the OB crew around him. He hated heights and yet would not complain about climbing the ladder to the top of a 150-foot television rostrum. He would just take a deep breath, clutch the ladder close to his chin, and slowly, very slowly, ascend the ladder to the top.

He liked the good things in life and enjoyed nothing more than to travel back to Euston from Manchester or Liverpool after a Saturday match, discussing over a four-course meal with a good bottle of wine the great or bad moments of the match. Ken's contract, which expired in September 1971, gave him first option on all soccer matches the BBC covered, live or recorded, including all the finals, the FA and the League Cup, the European and Cup Winners' Cup, the World Cup – everything in soccer. From 1969 we were covering two matches every Saturday in *Match of the Day*, and we were aware that in 1970 we would need three additional first-class commentators for other World Cup matches. In 1966 the only weakness in our World Cup coverage was in our commentating. Alan Weeks, Frank Bough and Wally Barnes all had to work fantastically hard to overcome their lack of match practice. They did a magnificent job but it would have helped if they had commented on a few matches beforehand. We all agreed, Dimmock, Cowgill and myself, that for 1970 we would have at least three experienced commentators, and we did: Ken Wolstenholme, David Coleman and Barry Davies, with Alan Weeks picking up the less important matches. By covering two matches in *MOTD* from 1969, with Ken always covering one, David Coleman and Barry Davies regularly kept their hand in. It was a very strong team.

David's greatest asset is his ability to reflect the feeling of the man on the terrace, together with his accurate identification and terrific ability to read a match. Also, he had, and still has, something that so few commentators have, the knowledge to know when not to talk. A lot still suffer with verbal diarrhoea.

Ken commentated on the 1970 World Cup Final between Italy and Brazil. But when everyone returned from Mexico the battle really started. The salary guarantee was pretty good for 1970. But Ken could expect double the basic with the hundreds of repeats, and with 10 per cent increase in the second and third years: plus all his private work – written articles, public appearances and after-dinner speaking – £25,000 would have been a comfortable estimate of his salary for that year, which was not bad for the early '70s. The best match guarantee that the corporation would come up with was a guaranteed 60 commentaries per year (Ken would normally do about 80 matches a year) and 3 finals a year from the following: FA Cup Final, European Cup Final, Cup Winners' Cup Final, UEFA Cup Final, European Championship and World Cup Final; plus any other soccer cup final we covered that year; also at least 3 internationals (Ken normally did 6).

Ken's agent, Teddy Summerfield, would not budge. It was one of the few mistakes he ever made. The 60 matches a year was not bad, neither was the financial side, but Teddy wanted a guarantee that Ken would cover every final in the book. This was where the big stumbling block appeared. The Summerfield Agency would not recognise that the Beeb had to have at least three active soccer commentators. So in September, when Ken's contract ran out, Bryan Cowgill called a special departmental meeting and announced it was impossible to reach agreement with Ken Wolstenholme's agent, and consequently Ken would not work for the BBC again. Very final, very dramatic. It's peculiar how ironic fate can often be. David Coleman took over the role of number-one soccer commentator.

104

Director and commentator share a drink after the World Cup Final, 1966.

But he was also introducing, editing and compiling *Sportsnight*, and by the following May, as the time of the 1972 FA Cup Final approached, he was uptight, a bag of nerves. David did the FA Cup Final and then disappeared for a complete rest. Barry Davies did practically everything else for the remainder of that season, which Ken would have picked up if he had been there. Dear Ken, he never deserved this break. BBC Television was poorer without his services.

PS: Twenty years later, in 1991, I was directing a match from Liverpool FC, one of those closed-circuit jobs where the pictures just went to a large screen at the visiting club, in this case, Millwall. Ken was the commentator. We hadn't met for 10 years and certainly hadn't worked together since his BBC departure in 1971. He was just about 70 and still over six feet, although slightly stooped with age; otherwise he didn't seem to have changed. We had lots to chat about and catch up on. Rehearsal with Ken was not necessary. In our time together we had covered hundreds of matches from Liverpool. About 2.30 Ken left the scanner and made his way up to the commentary point positioned high in the roof of the Main Stand. We had agreed Ken would start his commentary about five to three, just after Liverpool had trotted onto the pitch. This he did. He had only been going for a few seconds when a chill ran down my spine. It was as if time had stood still since 1966. His voice hadn't altered. It was just as young as 25 years earlier. Ken may have been 70 but his voice was that of a 45-year-old. Just as strong, just as beautiful. It was uncanny. Sometimes good things never change.

Chapter Seven

The Televising of the 1966 World Cup

The match programme of the 1966 World Cup.

By the early '60s competition between BBC and ITV was fearsome, not just programme-wise or contractual but physically. There were always the national events where our cameras and equipment operated side by side and force was used by one company or the other to make a point, gain an advantage.

But, in 1964 a BBC/ITV consortium was formed for the sole purpose of televising the World Cup. Neither organisation had enough equipment, manpower or facilities to tackle an event of this magnitude alone. It could only work if we split the coverage and the responsibilities and worked harmoniously together.

There were eight venues and the split was:

WEMBLEY we cover together, side by side
WHITE CITY one match only, ITV
ASTON VILLA ITV   MANCHESTER UNITED ITV
EVERTON BBC   SHEFFIELD WEDNESDAY BBC
SUNDERLAND ITV   MIDDLESBROUGH BBC

We, the consortium, had guaranteed FIFA that every match would be televised using electronic cameras. The above venues required 45 cameras. By 1964 we didn't have 45 outside broadcast cameras between us. Miles and miles of the 2-inch thick co-axle cable were wanted and also a thousand microphones for effects and commentary positions. More than 225 commentary positions had to be built, along with platforms for nearly 50 film cameras.

The broadcasting consortium just had to work. And it did. The two Executive Producers – Alan Chivers, BBC, Graham Turner, ITV – made sure of that. They were housed in the operation headquarters at TV Centre, Wood Lane where 500 visiting broadcasters made their base for those twenty days.

The day before the Opening Ceremony and Game, a briefing for all the production teams, producers, engineering managers, commentators and all the visiting 500, took place within the canteen of Television Centre, Wood Lane: 750 of us in total. We went right through the whole production, graphics, replays, etc so that every production would be similar. Then we were 'dismissed' to all venues, where we had some pretty experienced teams:

SHEFFIELD WEDNESDAY. Producer Ray Lakeland. Engineering Manager Fred Page. Commentator Alan Weeks. Group Two contained West Germany, Switzerland, Spain and Argentina and Alan Weeks pointed out, quite firmly, the robust tactics of Argentina and, exactly how good – and dangerous – were West Germany.

EVERTON. Producer Alan Mouncer. Engineering Manager Geoff Lomas. Commentator Walley Barnes. Group Three contained Bulgaria, Brazil, Hungary and Portugal. The best football in Round One came from Portugal (3) v Brazil (1), which gained an audience of 17 million.

MIDDLESBROUGH. Producer John McGonagle. Engineering Manager George Norton. Commentator Frank Bough. Group Four contained Russia, North Korea, Chile and Italy. The Koreans surprised everyone by reaching the quarter-finals. But without doubt the commentator's award should go to Frank Bough, who had the toughest pronunciation task in his very first match: Russia v North Korea!

As with all other Wembley matches, I stayed at the nearby hotel the night before the 1966 World Cup Final – The Hilton International, as it is now known. I was up and out early: I couldn't sleep. At 7 o'clock the hundreds of vendors around Wembley were opening up and laying out their stalls. Since 11th July Wembley had taken on a Hampstead Heath atmosphere of its own. Spivs and get-rich-quick boys were out in their hundreds. Stalls surrounded the stadium and ran the length of Olympic Way. One certain gentleman recorded all the BBC commentaries – off air – and quickly sold dozens of copies to the departing crowds. He now lives in his very luxurious farmhouse in South Devon.

As I walked around the stadium my mind took me through the various things that had happened since I had started to specialise in soccer coverage in 1964. We were worried that all World Cup matches must be covered by electronic cameras – not film, like in Chile in '62 – so we ran *Match of the Day* every Saturday on BBC2, mainly to give our outside-broadcast crews experience of televising soccer. Not having expected the programme to take off, we were all geared up to drop it in May '66. In a way, we did, transferring from BBC2 to BBC1.

In '64 our outside-broadcast crews would cover an opera one day, a church service another, and occasionally a soccer match. During those two years of '65 and '66 I built up a fantastic team of cameramen, sound and vision technicians and expert engineers. There were 54 at Wembley, and, for some, training reached Olympian proportions. All were great enthusiasts for soccer as well as being top craftsmen at their job. We positioned ourselves behind the Wembley South Stand. 'We' being all our vehicles, miles and miles of cable, every spare piece of electronic communication equipment invented, and midst all of this I had erected a Gardener's Hut in which we installed half a dozen phones, a TV monitor and the materials for making a pot of tea. This was our headquarters throughout the month of July. We had 10 cameras at Wembley, plus 19 effects microphones. Four cameras and six mics were at all other World Cup venues. I went hard and fast on my final team of 54 for Wembley way back in March, and we had worked together on every soccer match since. We knew each other's way of working so well. I gave each cameraman four sets of photos, postcard-size, of the four teams in the Wembley group, then more sets of other teams as we went into the quarters and semi-finals. I also insisted that the eight cameramen stayed at the Wembley hotel the night before all Wembley matches, including the Final, away from wives and girlfriends. Sex was banned.

I took the cameramen to the England training ground at Roehampton to stand on the touchline a few feet away from the England squad. Alf Ramsey and the players invited the lads into the dressing room. By the time 11th July came around they were treated by the players as personal friends. Of course they, all the crew, were nervous before the World Cup started, but I drummed it into their heads that when the excitement came, the goals, etc., they had to be ice cool. Indeed the control van was the quietest place at Wembley when those incidents happened. And it stayed like that throughout the final – until we came off the air.

Coverage at Wembley.

Alongside me I had the brilliant engineering managers Ted Bragg and Clive Potter. On ten cameras I had Maurice Abel, Harry Coventry, Keith Williams, Barry Chaston, Robin Sutherland, Selwyn Cox, Pete Cook, Ken Moir, Derek Wright and Ken Lane.

Their cameras were in the following places.

To obtain the 'outside' atmosphere one camera was positioned on the roof of a building, York House as it was called, 200 yards from the stadium at a lens height of 190 feet. This camera covered the crowd's arrival, the packed car parks, the programme and colour sellers, and, in addition, was able to zoom into the stadium to the crowded terraces behind one of the goals. The second camera was positioned outside the stadium on the balcony overlooking Olympic Way. It was along this tree-lined avenue that the fans poured into the stadium between 12.30 and 14.30. This camera was also used for interviews with VIPs and for the main linking of the film and build-up material after the start of transmission.

Inside the stadium the three main match cameras were positioned in line with the halfway line, in the stand opposite the Royal Box, the 'south' stand. Two of these cameras were on the special TV gantry slung from the roof of the main stand: one covered the pattern of the play, while the other covered the play in close-up – the player taking a free kick or throw, the attacking solo dribble, or the diving save by the goalkeeper. The third camera was positioned some 50 feet underneath the two main match cameras, in the midst of spectators; equipped with a special zoom, giving a range of lens from 8 inches to 80, its sole job was to obtain the 'personalities' – the forward shooting for goal, the offended or injured player – capturing in close-up, with split-second timing, the dramatic expressions of the individual players.

Another camera was positioned under the roof at the far end of the stadium and was able to produce panoramic shots of the stadium and the terraces packed with spectators.

The close-up shots of the Royal Box and presentation of the World Cup and medals required a further camera, located to one side and just in front of the Royal Box. To cover interviews after the match, and to provide the many captions required before and during the game, another camera was positioned in a specially constructed interview room just over the players' dressing room.

Two further cameras were used on the pitch itself, both hand-held radio cameras. Their coverage enabled the viewers to see the players lining up in the players' tunnel, close-ups of the pre-match presentation and toss-up, crowd close-ups, and the memorable victory lap of honour, when players were surrounded by team reserves, officials and a score or two of press photographers.

On that day we had 42 commentary positions for television, and across the other side of Wembley another 35 for radio. Our transmission went live to 48 countries, including Australia and New Zealand, South Africa, North America, all of South America and, of course, every European country one could think of. Videotape

111

and film was flown out of Heathrow to the Middle East and the whole of Africa throughout the night. Thirty-two million watched the Final in this country and a further 30 million abroad, which, for 1966, was going some, setting a TV audience record.

Two weeks before the start of the World Cup the BBC obtained its first slow-motion-stop-action machine. It cost the BBC £58,000, a lot of money in '66. Now this would really 'lift' our coverage. Its use was never fully exploited. Three sound and vision lines were 'radio-linked' from a position high at Wembley Stadium to the TV Centre at Shepherds Bush. Two of these three circuits carried the complete transmission picture, the output of my master control van. This was a complete safety-first operation, i.e. belt-and-braces: within seconds of one line failing the other would be transmitted. Remembers this was the Sixties.

I had decided the third link would carry the output of camera five, the camera high up behind one goal, or the output of one of the two cameras, positioned low and close behind each goal. But, it had been decided that our revolutionary machine was too valuable to be let loose at an Outside Broadcast, and would be based and operated from TV Centre, where inexperience throughout the duration of the World Cup just repeated each goal from the normal camera position, not from an isolated camera which we are used to seeing nowadays. We lost the opportunity of showing the world of viewers every goal from a different angle.

Even when we had arrived at Wembley, about 10 days before the World Cup was to start, we still had our problems. On 1st July, the very day we arrived at the stadium to rig up our 22 miles of cable, a big bombshell hit us – or me, in actual fact. The FA had arranged for bands at all the grounds to play in the arenas before the matches, at half-time, and following the final whistle. We, television, were all geared up to cover the bands in our transmission, especially those going worldwide. For years the atmosphere between the Musicians' Union and the BBC had not been healthy. Wild-cat strikes or arguments were always taking place. On 1st July the Musicians' Union hit the Beeb right between the eyes (or ears). If we featured the bands at any time during our transmission we were to pay the equivalent of £10 per bandsman, £20 if the transmission went abroad, live or recorded. At every ground the military bands numbered about 50 or 60, apart from the opening ceremony and final at Wembley, when the massed bands of the Brigade of Guards would be playing in the presence of Her Majesty Queen Elizabeth – all 278 of them! We just could not afford to pay the Musicians' Union's rates. They would have added £78,000 to our broadcasting bill, the equivalent to £2 million today. I broke the news to all the other TV directors. I was feeling very annoyed.

I spent all night poring over contracts, broadcasting regulations, etc. Then I spotted something. No monies would have to be paid to any union, band, etc., if the band in question was appearing at the royal command of Her Majesty. I contacted Major 'Jig' Jaeger, the Senior Director of Music of the Brigade of Guards, and also the Director of Music of the Irish Guards. I told him of the spot of bother we were in. Now, 'Jig' realised the impact of television, especially with our transmission going to all those countries abroad. Together we drafted out a couple of paragraphs. On 3rd July, he dashed down to Windsor Castle, where Her Majesty happened to be that day. Five hours later, he reappeared waving the magic paper, with signature, in his hand. It was as follows: HER MAJESTY, QUEEN ELIZABETH, COMMANDS THE MASSED BANDS OF THE BRIGADE OF GUARDS TO PERFORM IN HER PRESENCE ON 11TH JULY AND 30TH JULY AT WEMBLEY STADIUM.

The Musicians' Union could do nothing. Therefore, on those two occasions, viewers at home and abroad saw and heard, before the match and at half-time, the massed bands of the Brigade of Guards. They were the only bands performing at World Cup grounds that were actually seen on television. I am proud of my country and heritage and was determined the world would see us at our best.

On Friday, 8th July, before the opening ceremony on Monday, 11th July, the FA had arranged a complete rehearsal. Her Majesty the Queen would be standing on a small podium/rostrum alongside the track, together with three or four FIFA dignitaries. In the middle of the arena would be the combined bands of the Brigade of Guards, and on cue a procession would march from the players' tunnel, made up of 16 groups of 15 Boy Scouts, each group dressed in the playing kit of one of the participating countries, preceded by the national flag of that country and a banner bearing the country's name. Now the organisers, the Football Association, are without doubt the greatest politicians within the world of football, but promoters and showbiz producers they are not!

A complete dress rehearsal took place on this Friday with someone standing in for HM and the full massed bands of the Brigade of

Guards really thundering out. Then the procession started. It was a shambles, a gigantic shambles – and that is to praise it. It was repeated after tea and was an even bigger shambles. So George Stanton, Wembley's General Manager, had a word or two with the FA officials, some six of whom had been standing watching. They disappeared, delighted to hand over responsibility for the opening ceremony to George Stanton. George conferred with 'Jig' Jaeger, and within 10 minutes there appeared one of the biggest regimental sergeant majors the Guards had ever produced. And he had a voice to go with his size. He set to work with these groups

1966 World Cup
Opening Ceremony
Wembley

Shots taken from BBC1 transmission of the opening ceremony of the
1966 World Cup.

of Boy Scouts. The shamble became a saunter, the saunter a walk, the walk a march. Afternoon turned into evening, so at 10 o'clock the following day it started all over again. There were tears, there were sore feet, but all the time this voice thundered out throughout the stadium, this time with the help of a big bass drum. On the Monday, when the opening ceremony took place and the time came for these lads to march into the stadium, I can assure you that they did the Guards proud, backs straight, all marching in step, arms swinging backward and forward, and, if you listened very carefully above the cheering of one hundred thousand spectators and the magnificent sound of the Brigade of Guards band, you could hear, coming from the players' tunnel, from where these Boy Scouts had marched on, 'Left, right, left, right, keep your head up', etc., etc.

After every match I kept my own diary of events:

Monday July 11th. Coverage of the opening ceremony was OK. I felt as the transmission went on that this was turning out to be the perfect warm-up for the match. I was wrong. ENGLAND 0 URUGUAY 0. A dull boring match and our coverage was just as

Cameraman operating from the TV gantry at Wembley.

115

bad; master camera too wide. Close-ups were too slow. Nerves got the better of the crew. Cameraman Keith Williams, operating camera three (close-up camera) over Exit 37 had to work almost bent double. For an hour and a half was one thing but the extra hour of the Opening Ceremony left him stuck bent double on the final whistle. BBC doctor arranged his transfer to Harley Street's London Clinic for two nights' occupation, non-stop physiotherapy. He turned up at Wembley two days later, walking like a guardsman.

Wednesday 13th. Kick Off 7.30. FRANCE 1 MEXICO 1. Crowd 55,000. Sound on the ball this time. John Livingston, the sound operator, moved his hands over the controls as if he was playing a piano. Camera work was much better. Couldn't have been worse.

Saturday 16th. Kick Off 7.30. MEXICO 0 ENGLAND 2. Crowd 85,000. Sound milked this dry. Magnificent. Camera work sharper. Faster onto the close-ups. Lads are now into their stride.

Tuesday 19th. Kick Off 4.30. MEXICO 0 URUGUAY 0. Poor crowd of 45,000. Rained throughout this dull game. It's very difficult getting the lads to 'stay with it', keep on their toes. Kept on repeating on talk-back 'any moment now it will explode'.

Wednesday 20th. Kick Off 7.30. FRANCE 0 ENGLAND 2. Crowd of 92,000 provided a back-cloth for our coverage. Sound never missed a trick. All cameras clicking along very smoothly. Now this was good. We're into our stride.

Saturday 23rd. Quarter-Finals. Kick Off 3.00. ENGLAND 1 ARGENTINA 0. Crowd 85,000. A warm sunny day. This was the dirtiest game of football I have ever covered. 75 per cent of the antics of the South Americans was never transmitted. I never transmitted the output of the particular camera that covered the fouls: hair pulling, tripping, spitting, shirt pulling, jabbing two fingers into the eyes when the referee was not looking. Jimmy Hill, our summariser for this match, was magnificent, he spotted the Argentines' tactics within five minutes of kick-off. I transmitted 10 per cent of the dirty tactics. In the interview room afterwards, Alf Ramsey referred to the Argentina players as 'animals'. Which they were. But, our coverage is nearing perfection.

Tuesday 26th. Semi-Final. Kick Off 7.30. Crowd 90,000. ENGLAND 2 PORTUGAL 0. The finest game of football I have seen and our coverage lived up to that standard. Twenty minutes before the first foul. Slight camera fault on two. Repaired within seconds. All cameras really trying various shots. Working, working all the time. Offering shots, making my job easy.

Thursday 28th. Match for 3rd/4th place. Kick Off 7.30. PORTUGAL 2 USSR 1. Crowd 70,000. Wide angle is now working to a pattern. Speed of 'personality cameras' is terrific. Everyone is now ready for the 'big one'.

About twenty of the team stayed overnight at the York House Hotel. Nevertheless, sleep deserted me the night before the final and, by seven o'clock, I found myself wandering around the stadium precincts, which were becoming quite active. The stallholders were already putting out their produce. The roads and pavements were being swept and washed, as were the stadium corridors and steps. Groundsman Percy Fuller and his half dozen staff were going over the magnificent pitch first of all on hands and knees removing any resemblance of a weed then with mower and roller. An army of 'Mrs Mopps' had dusted all 98,000 seats the day before. By eight o'clock vans were queueing in the three big tunnels unloading their produce for the kitchens and bars. The coaches carrying the brilliantly dressed guardsmen were beginning to arrive outside the players' tunnel.

All this activity would have made a brilliant television feature on its own.

Small isolated pockets of chanting fans were steadily arriving in the surrounding streets. When our vehicles had arrived to 'rig-in' on July 1st and were located within a high secured fence behind the South Stand, this area became known as the 'Television Compound' and three security guards were allocated to protect our area. With each match security numbers increased to reach a dozen by two days before the final, when they were then joined by a dozen uniformed police. As it turned out we certainly needed them in the 5–6 hours leading up to the kick-off. Every trick possible was tried to get into the TV Compound. Climbing, jumping, rushing, pushing, forgery, written letters on gold-headed paper, phone calls; you name it – they tried it. The cheekiest was played at about two o'clock, when a very smartly dressed gentleman, with his wife and four daughters, presented themselves to the security at our TV compound, identified themselves as 'Herr Willy Brand, the Mayor of West Berlin, and his family' and asked me to conduct them to their commentary box. I had just started our transmissions to overseas viewers. That to me was important. For the next hour

117

this charade was carried out, then he and his so-called family disappeared!

And so to Saturday, 30th July. The 1966 World Cup Final. England versus West Germany. We were transmitting from 11.30 to, eventually, 6.15.

I was quite surprised how detached I felt, indeed, how calm all the members of our team seemed. We had a team wearing white shirts and a team wearing red shirts. In spite of the electric atmosphere, which invaded not only the stadium but the television platform housing the world's commentators and technicians, and a host of cameras, our team were ice cool. Ice cool and razor sharp. That team, our team, were also magnificent that day. The crowd were chanting either 'Uwe, Uwe' (Uwe Seeler, Germany's favourite player), or, and much more loudly, 'England, England'. A Brazilian supporter, by now recovered from the disappointment he had suffered when his own beloved country was defeated, sportingly came along to beat in time with his drums, as if the match was being played at the Maracana Stadium in Rio.

Our sound technicians found him; indeed, they seemed to find everyone. They surpassed themselves that day, working on one of those very complicated sound-mixing desks, as if they were playing a Wurlitzer organ. The sound was so magnificent that one felt one was leaning over the parapet of a huge building, being drawn not by a void but by the noise of the crowd. Ken Wolstenholme was also magnificent that day and would have been the first to agree that TV production is a team event, never more so than with a football production. The producer, the cameramen, the commentator, each of us following the others and dovetailing together. By the time 3 o'clock came, the temperature in our *non*-air-conditioned 1966 control van had reached 90 degrees. Sweat just rolled off us for the next four hours.

Haller scored first for West Germany, but dejection did not enter into the voice of Ken Wolstenholme, only optimism, practically elation, because he reminded viewers that in previous World Cup Finals the teams scoring first had actually lost the match; so although our pictures showed the elation of the West German players, his words cheered up millions of disappointed Englishmen.

Half-time, and we were about 3 minutes into the magnificent sight and sound of the marching display by the Brigade of Guards.

118

30th July 1966, the teams line up before the match in front of a capacity Wembley Stadium
© EMPICS

The ref tosses the coin as the captains meet.

© EMPICS

After just thirteen minutes West Germany score with a goal by Haller, 0–1.

© EMPICS

The phone rang. It was the Head of Sport speaking from master control back at TV Centre. 'Alec, all is going well...' I waited for the real reason for the phone call. 'We've had a request from the Prime Minister's Office.' The PM at this very moment was sitting in the Royal Enclosure across the other side of the stadium. I know this for a fact because I had just 'punched-up' a shot of him as the band marched in.

'The Prime Minister is quite prepared to speak to the nation during this half-time break...' My heart sank. I knew what was coming. '...I informed his office that you, the Producer, must make this decision.' I thought of all the effort to get permission to televise the band; I could imagine the reaction within the million of homes for this magnificent sight to be replaced by a talking head. My reply was short.

'No. Camera Two, hold that shot of the trombones. On Two.' The phone line went dead.

I realised that my decision would not get me any brownie-points.

There were moments when ice-cold neutral brains nearly got involved with the emotional Wembley crowd: during the penalising of Jackie Charlton, for instance, and when West Germany equalised seconds from the end of normal time. 'OK, lads, take a deep breath. Relax,' I said. 'Another 30 minutes of football after 25 hours of transmissions will not kill us.'

Then those awful minutes – impossible to think it was only seconds – of waiting as the Swiss referee, Gottfried Dienst, consulted his Russian linesman, Tojik Bakhramov, about England's third, and really decisive, goal. When the ball hit the crossbar and bounced back onto the pitch, was it still in play or had it crossed the line for a goal? The Russian nodded. 'A goal,' signalled Dienst, and England roared.

And then, just about 5.20 pm, on that warm July afternoon, in a street-deserted country, with England leading Germany 3–2, Kenneth Wolstenholme begins to build up his commentary for the last 30 seconds of the 1966 World Cup Final.

Wolstenholme: *'The referee looks at his watch ... any second now it could be all over.'*

Ray Wilson, in the England half, passes the ball to Bobby Moore.

'There's thirty seconds by our watch, the Germans are going down ... they can hardly stand up.'

Six minutes later
Geoff Hurst equalises
for England, 1–1.

© EMPICS

With only 12
minutes of the
match left to play
Martin Peters
scores and England
go 2–1 up.

© EMPICS

But a scrambled
goal from West
Germany's
Wolfgang Weber
just before the
final whistle
forced the game
into extra time.

© EMPICS

Referee Dienst, whistle in his mouth looks at his watch. Then waves play on.

'It's all over, I think ... no ... it's...'

Bobby Moore floats the ball into the German half ... to Geoff Hurst.

Wolstenholme utters the famous words *'and here comes Hurst.'*

Geoff Hurst collects the ball from Moore ... and moves toward the German goal.

'He's got ... some people are on the pitch ... they think it's all over.'

Geoff Hurst volleys with his left foot and scores his third. England's fourth.

'IT IS NOW.'

Hurst turns and runs toward Alan Ball, arms outstretched.

'It's four.'

What follows is like a photo shutter clicking in my mind: Jackie Charlton on his knees on the final whistle with his face turned towards heaven; slim, young, good-looking Bobby Moore collecting the World Cup from Her Majesty the Queen, and my favourite shot, right in front of our television gantry, little Nobby Stiles, his front dentures removed, skipping down the touchline with the cup held aloft in his right arm, his protruding fangs opened in the widest grin of the day. 'Ey-I-Adio, We've won the Cup.'

We were working until about 7.30 p.m. There were masses of interviews and reports to transmit to various countries. When we had finally finished I just walked around the inside of the stadium. Alone, I looked up into the familiar huge girders that, two hours earlier, were vibrating with the thunderous roaring ... 'England ... England ... England'. The wind was blowing the paper cups around; the stadium seemed to be talking to itself.

Our team, the lads, my crew of 54, had been brilliant: one could tell they were proud of what they had achieved. Not missing a shot, a sound, a trick; always anticipating what was required: a shouting player, a formation of play, a hefty tackle or the thunderous roaring of the respective fans. Some got so caught up with the excitement of the occasion that they stayed manning their camera for more than seven hours. The event was so fantastically exhilarating because this was where one transposed every sound and movement to millions of homes throughout the world.

122

Geoff Hurst shoots, hits the underside of the crossbar and goes over the line, or did it?

© EMPICS

Bobby Charlton appeals to the Swiss referee Gottfried Dienst that it did cross the line.   © EMPICS

Alf Ramsey (Manager) and Harold Sheperdson (Trainer) feel the tension on the bench as the referee and linesman debate if it crossed the line or not.   © EMPICS

After consulting the Russian linesman Tofik Bakhramov the referee agrees and the goal stands, 3–2 to England.

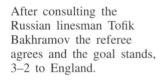

© British Pathe

123

Prior to the World Cup the American networks had always been regarded by the television world as the top for sports coverage. Our World Cup coverage changed all that. For several years to come, certainly way into the mid-70s, BBC's Outside Broadcast Department had a steady stream of foreign production and technical staff wanting to know 'how' we did it.

In that, now deserted, windy stadium I thought back several months and to all the hard work that had gone into this day. Now it was all over. But never to be forgotten.

I, together with half a dozen cameramen, started to make my way to Shepherd's Bush and Television Centre, where most of us had left our cars. There were hundreds of parties going on between Wembley and Shepherd's Bush, especially in Kensington. The doors were opened when the hosts realised what we had done; we had a few drinks and just moved on to the next party. We reached Television Centre at 5.30 a.m.!

Two disappointments. We should have televised the 1966 World Cup in colour, but the manufacturers had brought great pressure to bear on the government of the day not to allow colour TV within the UK until June 1967 – Wimbledon. Politics won. In 1970 Mexico, a so-called backward television country, televised the World Cup in colour.

Secondly, Europe – EBU (the European Broadcasting Union) decided that a church service from Rome was the 'Best Outside Broadcast of 1966' ...

Extra time

I very nearly got away without answering THE question. Whilst I attend to it, you go and get out that dusty video of the 1966 World Cup Final. No matter who or where you are, whenever the '66 Final is discussed someone will ask, 'Was it a goal?', 'Was the ball for England's third goal over the line?' Start spooling through the video until nine minutes into extra time. Now run it at normal speed.

Nobby Stiles, centre, near the halfway line, has the ball and passes to Alan Ball, who takes it up the right wing, well into the West German half. He chips the ball over to Geoff Hurst, who brings it down with his right, swivels, and slams the ball, hard, beyond goalkeeper Tilkowski's outstretched arms.

Some people are on the pitch ... they think its all over ...
Geoff Hurst slams in England's 4th goal to become the first player to score a hat-trick in a World Cup Final, 4–2.

© EMPICS

The Queen presents Bobby Moore with the Jules Rimet Trophy, England are World Champtions.

© EMPICS

Bobby Moore holds the trophy aloft as the team celebrate.

© EMPICS

125

England's 1966 World Cup winning team.

The ball hits the crossbar and bounces down behind the goalkeeper. Referee Dienst cannot see exactly where the ball lands. The German goalkeeper obscures the ball. But another red-shirted player is charging up whilst all this has been happening, number 21, Roger Hunt of Liverpool and England. He and he alone had a perfect view of the ball landing behind the goalkeeper. He was 12 feet from the goal line and could see right behind the goalkeeper. Within a split second of that ball hitting the ground his arms are raised, instinctively, and he's wheeling around to celebrate the goal with Geoff Hurst. Of all the people on the pitch that afternoon, Roger Hunt had the most perfect view of that goal.

Now press the 'go slow' button on the video control. See what I mean?

England three, West Germany two.

Every so often extracts of that World Cup Final appear and no matter where I am I still get worked up over that third disputed goal. But it's good that we can still celebrate that fantastic victory and that, even now, forty years later, it is still the most watched TV broadcast in British history. A gigantic audience of 32.3 million tuned in to see England's 4–2 victory over West Germany. This is all the more unusual because in 1966 only 15 million homes had TV sets, compared to the 24 million homes that are now equipped.

The British Film Institute recently issued a list of the top TV transmissions over the years:

1.	The 1966 World Cup Final	32.3 million
2.	Funeral of Princess Diana, 1997	32.1 million
6.	FA Cup Final Replay, Chelsea v Leeds, 1970	28.49 million
14.	Winter Olympics, Torvill & Dean, 1994	23.95 million

I doubt that the '66 figure will ever be surpassed because forty years ago there were just three channels. Nowadays there are hundreds to choose from.

Chapter Eight

The Axeman Cometh

The place was Liverpool Football Club. The date, April 1967.

In those days whenever covering a match at Anfield we would park our vehicles, all five of them, in Kemlyn Road, run the cables down an alleyway that ran between rows of two-up two-down houses, then over a brick wall and straight up to the TV gantry, which was positioned at the rear of the Kemlyn Road Stand.

That's what we had been doing for the past four years, and even though Liverpool FC were starting to expand their main grandstand on the opposite side of the ground, to include a television gantry, it would not be ready for at least another two years.

And so it was that on this particular day all the cables had been run out over the wall and into the ground to their various cameras and other pieces of equipment. All the equipment had been tested and rehearsals had taken place. Bill Shankly had been quizzed and had announced his team to all and sundry.

The Kop had sung their anthem, 'You'll Never Walk Alone', accompanied by a human mass of scarves, flags, ribbons, all in red and white. In those days, the '60s and '70s, that picture at eighteen minutes to three was a sight to behold. Having seen it once you would want to tell your grandchildren about it years later.

The teams had run onto the pitch just as 'You'll Never Walk Alone' came to an end. Everything was building up to the kick-off. Down in the scanner, I had recorded the opening of the match. Everyone in the business knew it would be based on the rendering of the Kop anthem. I also knew how to cash in on a good thing when I saw it.

The referee was just calling the two captains together for the toss-up. It was four minutes to kick-off.

Just then there was a loud thumping on the control-room door.

A very loud thumping. My senior engineer went and answered it, only to return a few seconds later, saying that a fellow outside was asking to see me.

'Look, we're about to kick off,' I protested, at the same time leaving my seat at the control desk just to tell this man to come back later. Much later.

The fellow standing outside was big, about six foot, thickset, dressed in overalls and trainers. There was one other thing about him: He was carrying the biggest axe I had ever seen. His arm was stretched out straight. The axe handle ran from his fingers and finished in a big axe-head resting on his shoulder. 'Your cables are running over my wall. I want them removed. At once.' As he spoke he tapped the axe-head against his shoulder as if to emphasise each word. It was quite menacing.

'On every visit,' I replied, 'our cables run over your wall, and they have done for four years.'

'Well, bloody well remove them,' he said in his broad Scouse accent. 'Either you remove them or I'll bloody well remove them myself.' With this, and so saying, he raised the axe in the air and waved it about.

Knowing I would get no mercy from this Liverpudlian Al Capone I verbally sallied forth. Within a second he joined me so that both of us were voicing our thoughts, him in a broad Scouse accent, me as a Londoner. We were not pontificating about the quality of the air in the north-west. Around us the air was blue. And that's an understatement. It has been said that, despite there being 40,000 cheering fans within 25 yards of us, our conversation could be clearly heard and understood!

Though I was standing on the top step of our scanner, the sight of this fellow waving this axe around as if it was a football rattle and screaming abuse made me begin to realise I was fighting a losing battle.

Suddenly in the middle of this bedlam – and don't forget I was still attempting to give as good as I was getting – I heard him utter the word 'negotiate'.

I shut up for a second. Then, 'How much?' I yelled.

He also shut up. Pause. 'A fiver,' he shouted.

My hand flew to my back pocket. Out came a fiver. Out, just as quickly, came his hand. He had taken a step backwards and was turning around, the sun just glinting on the axe-head, before I had dropped my arm. I turned, took a step backwards into the scanner; slammed the door shut; turned toward the camera controls, sliding into my seat and glancing up at the dozen or so monitors facing me. The referee was just placing his whistle in his mouth for the kick-off. We were back in business.

I realise, now, that everything has a pattern. The animals of the wild have a pattern. The lions, the elephants, the wildebeest always come back to a familiar hunting ground each year; so also do David Attenborough's gorillas. And like the gorillas of the wild, so also did our axeman from Liverpool. So started a custom, a habit, that was to remain the same for at least the next three years. Five pounds became six. Twenty-six became twenty-seven. Thirty-seven became thirty-eight.

With each returning visit to Anfield the ante went up by one pound, and I can assure you that in '67, '68 and '69 we made many, many visits to Anfield and Liverpool FC. Al Capone still lived – this was protection money.

He was much more amicable on our return visits. He would come knocking on the scanner door at about 12.30 p.m. for a Saturday 3.00 p.m. kick-off, or 5.30 p.m. for an evening kick-off. But he always carried his bloody axe in his hand.

By the '70s our gratuity payment was in the 40s. We pleaded with him. We begged him. We threatened him. Some of the crew would proposition him, even trying to seduce his wife. All to no avail. Then one day that lovely new grandstand that Liverpool FC had been building on the opposite side was completed and in its roof was a lovely shining camera and commentary platform. We mentally put two fingers into a salute to our axeman and moved our cables, vehicles and equipment over to the other side of the ground. Never again would we have to run our cables down the alleyway and over Mr Axeman's wall.

We had been in this new position about a couple of months. It was a Saturday morning and I had just run through the cameras and checked everything with the crew when there was a very loud banging on the scanner door.

I opened it. Standing there was a very flushed club secretary, as he was then called, Peter Robinson. Very flushed and with a fistful of papers in each hand.

'These arrived this morning, Alec,' Peter explained, waving papers in the air in a very agitated manner. 'We're being sued,' he shouted.

'Who are? By whom? What for?' I asked.

"You, Alec Weeks. Me, Peter Robinson. Liverpool Football Club. The BBC.'

'Who by?'

'Mr—— the axeman,' said Peter.

'What for? We never put a glove on him,' I shouted.

'LOSS OF EARNINGS!' screamed an exasperated Club Secretary.

Directing *Match of the Day* from outside broadcast control van, 1970.

© Reveille Newspapers Ltd.

Chapter Nine

Mexico and Back Again – 1970-86

Since 1966 our mail from dissatisfied viewers had increased considerably, all directed at the standard of commentary. David Coleman, whilst holidaying on a Spanish beach in 1968, came up with the answer. It was called, 'So You Want To Be A Commentator?'

Anyone who fancied their chances at being a commentator would be heard and the eventual winner would join our commentary team in Mexico. All this was staged within the weekly *Sportsnight with Coleman* programme. The letters came in by the sackful, just under 5,000 of them. The obvious ones were soon eliminated: the six-year-old boy; the 92-year-old fan; the female sex. Women's Lib had not established itself in 1968/9. All the BBC regions were also included in the competition.

First, individual cassettes were requested; this certainly gave us a clue as to the subject's standard of elocution, pronunciation, and whether he possessed a good or bad voice. At this stage there were 1,200 hopefuls.

The next stage, in April 1969, was for 400 auditionees to visit our regional studios in Cardiff, Bristol, Glasgow, Manchester, Birmingham, Belfast, and, of course, London to give commentary to a five-minute piece of filmed soccer action. This certainly split the men from the boys and reduced the field to 30.

The remaining field did not just include the loyal soccer fan, or the avid television sports viewer, but professional soccer players, managers, and experienced broadcasters and actors, all of whom attended a studio in London to give a commentary on the previous day's Northern Ireland v. England match, which had been transmitted live. This was on 4th May. On the following Wednesday, 7th May, we selected 12 from the 30 and sent our would-be commentators to Wembley Stadium.

And so at Wembley Stadium on a fairly chilly May evening, when we were covering live the England v. Wales home international, these 12, who had slogged their way through all our tests, reached their penultimate hurdle. They commentated on the whole of the match, only this time their recorded commentaries were listened to by our panel of judges: Bryan Cowgill, Head of Sport, BBC Television; Sir Alf Ramsey, England Football Manager; the Rt Hon Dennis Howell, Minister of Sport; Tony Book, captain of Manchester City FC. And from the twelve we selected a final six to appear in our *Sportsnight* studio on 22nd May 1969. They were: Ed Stewart, then a 28-year-old disc jockey on *Children's Favourites*; Larry Canning, aged 42, a Scot living in Birmingham, an ex-Aston Villa wing half; Tony Adamson, a 29-year-old hospital broadcaster from Belfast; Idwal Robling, a 42-year-old Welsh amateur international, and the manager of a sweet factory; Gerry Harrison, aged 32, an ex-Oxford Blue and senior amateur player, working for BBC Radio Merseyside; and Ian St John, aged 30, a professional player since 18, 21 caps for Scotland, who still played for Liverpool and was already a broadcaster on BBC Radio Merseyside.

Watching the programme it became clear it would be between four runners: Idwal Robling, Ian St John, Ed Stewart and Gerry Harrison. Having spoken to each of the competitors individually at Wembley when they gave their final commentary, my money was on Ian St John. He had worked really hard for this and had all the potential requirements of a soccer commentator. The results were announced within *Sportsnight* by Bryan Cowgill: fourth – Ed Stewart; third – Gerry Harrison; second – Ian St John; and first – Idwal Robling from Wales.

I just could not agree with the result. I felt the Scotsman, Ian St John, was good – very, very good. Indeed, later that evening, following the Wales/England international, when I had heard all the tapes, Ian St John stood out so clearly in his delivery and his knowledge of the game that I was itching to 'get to him' to polish up his rough edges. The only fault he had was his accent. Anyone south of Crewe would have difficulty understanding him when he got excited and raised the pitch and tempo of his voice. That was correctable. It seemed that Sir Alf Ramsey would not have Ian St John at any price: he threatened withdrawing from the panel, a walkout, even a lack of cooperation at the Mexico World Cup in a year's time. So the rest of the judging panel capitulated, and Ian St John was made runner-up.

Over the years I have often wondered how life, indeed lives, would have been different if Ian St John had joined the BBC's soccer commentary team of Coleman, Wolstenholme and Davies. Even to this day there are some who do not realise how close they were to being 'not wanted on the voyage'.

So Idwal Robling went to Mexico as a member of the BBC's commentary team and commentated on three matches. He returned to his native Wales, where he became a popular commentator and reporter on BBC Wales sports programmes, both TV and radio.

We should have overruled Sir Alf and let him walk out if he wanted to, but we were afraid of his lack of cooperation in Mexico. The BBC lost a good commentator.

Ian St John persevered and eventually, from 1981, was ITV's permanent anchorman for their *On The Ball* programme and a regular contributor to all ITV's soccer programmes. Gerry Harrison is now, and has been for 20 years, one of ITV's top soccer commentators. Ed Stewart is an experienced broadcaster, but still an Everton fan! Well, we can't all be perfect!

So, in spite of the effort and the cost, the BBC's sports department of 1969 never really obtained any benefits from its labours; I often felt that we never really bothered to.

All this was part of the build-up to our coverage of the 1970 Mexico World Cup. In my opinion England had a greater, stronger team than in 1966.

I have a confession to make – I was primarily responsible for introducing the 'disease' of TV soccer, i.e. the expert. The ex-footballer who pontificates for what seems like hours on end before a match and talks non-stop after the final whistle. Sure, we've always had 'summarisers' sitting alongside the commentators, ready to explode for a minute or two at half time, but, after the '66 World Cup both BBC and ITV went mad. If we had two summarisers alongside the commentator, ITV would have three. For the next World Cup or European Championships they would have four, so we would increase our number to five. It became out of control.

Back to 1970. Mexico. With our team we took out Don Revie and Joe Mercer, both fine international players and now experienced managers of First Division Clubs. They were to comment during the matches and be interviewed each day by David Coleman. Now Mexican television transmitted the '70 World Cup in colour, but down in Guadalajara their studio equipment was still basic; no zooms, no colour. Now our Studio Director, Jonathan Martin, had come straight from Lime Grove Studios and from directing 1970s-style cameras, in colour, with zoom lenses. So the interviews with our two experts, which were transmitted straight onto the satellite to London, were filmed with Turrett Lenses.

One interview got under way and all was being received satisfactorily in London. Jonathan had two cameras, one on Don and the other on Joe. In the Gallery alongside him Jonathan had an interpreter who would translate everything that he uttered. 'Track in, Camera One . . .' says Jonathan. The interpreter translates. Coleman was building the interview into a healthy discussion on English tactics. Jonathan repeats his instruction, this time to the other camera, '. . . Track in, Camera Two.' And so on, gradually tracking the cameras closer and closer to his two experts, aiming, of course, to obtain the brilliant close-ups that were part of *Sportsnight with Coleman*. Bit by bit, he slowly pushed the cameras closer, stopping Don Revie's eighteen inches away, but he was still not satisfied with the close-up of 'uncle' Joe, as he was affectionately known. '. . . Tighter . . . Closer . . . push in, Camera One . . .'

Now cool, calm, passive Joe Mercer may have given in his day many co-operative interviews to the media, but none which included a camera like this Mexican Monster. He wasn't just worried. He was terrified. His face and neck were turning bright red. Beads of perspiration were gathering on his forehead, running down and dripping off his nose. His eyes took on a startled look as the lens was now just a few inches from his face. His hands were turning white while he squeezed the arms of his chair. Certain that the monster was about to devour him he slipped lower and lower in his chair, all coherent speech being reduced to mumbling and occasional groans of anguish.

In the Gallery Jonathan still called for a closer shot, the interpreter translating every word with clear Spanish diction. Then Coleman exploded as only he could.

'Jonathan. What the ******* hell do you think you are doing? You are frightening poor Joe here to ****** death. Now get these ******* cameras away. You're not in London now.'

But London had seen and recorded all this.

Copies are still being made.

I based myself in Guadalajara, where England were playing their first-round matches. The players were in terrific form, and had been since the so-called 'stolen bracelet' affair, involving Bobby Moore, in Bogota, Colombia, four weeks earlier.

During that incident, I had been staying with the team in Bogota's Tequendama Hotel, and Monday morning found me sitting on the settee in the hotel foyer next to Jackie Charlton and Alan Mullery. Suddenly one of the lads, Martin Peters I think it was, ran towards us and shouted hoarsely: 'Bobby's been arrested and accused of stealing a ring.'

Now Jackie, thinking it was 'Our Bobby', his brother, suddenly took off like one possessed; but it was Bobby Moore, England's team captain, who had been accused, not Bobby Charlton. The two Bobbies had been idling away their time looking for a suitable present for Bobby Charlton's wife when one Clara Padilla accused Moore of stealing a bracelet from the hotel jewellers'. Police appeared on the scene within seconds and the England team captain was placed under open arrest.

The England team flew on to Mexico without him. Moore remained in Colombia for 11 days; but his capacity for diplomacy rose above these trumped-up charges, and on 30th May, half a stone lighter, he rejoined his colleagues in Guadalajara. The majority of stars would have quietly paid the blackmail money demanded to avoid this international incident, which is what it became; the majority of Colombian people felt that Moore was the latest victim of several notorious attempts to frame visiting celebrities into paying the costs of alleged thefts. But it was only a conditional release. It was not until 2nd December 1975 that the Legal Justice of Colombia considered the case 'closed for all practical purposes'.

It was Bobby Moore OBE who led the England side out, on 2nd June 1970, in the Guadalajara Stadium for England's first game in defence of their World Cup, against Romania.

In England's third match, at midday on Sunday, 7th June, under a white-hot Mexican sun, they lost one-nil to Brazil. Without a doubt, England were brilliant, and that evening at our reception of the Hilton Hotel, where we and the England squad were staying, the effervescent Nobby Stiles was confidence itself. 'We've tested them. We know their weaknesses. We'll beat them in the final.'

In the meantime, they just had a little match to play, in León, against West Germany. They had beaten them at Wembley in 1966 (and, I always add, also in 1918 and 1945), so why not now? Everything was going according to plan, with England leading two-nil with twenty minutes left to play – and this without Gordon Banks, mysteriously hit with severe stomach problems. I was sitting 50 feet from the touchline, mentally sorting out our move back to Mexico City for the semi-final. Alf Ramsey had substituted Bobby Charlton, to rest him for the semi-final against Italy in three days' time when bingo, or rather Bonetti!

We lost 3–2. How? Why? Who will ever know? What I do know is that Peter Bonetti would have stopped two of the three goals scored against him at any other time, but not on this Sunday, 14th June. Bobby Charlton had been keeping Beckenbauer completely occupied, but with Charlton substituted Beckenbauer masterminded the great West German comeback.

In spite of all that has been said and written about England and the Mexico 1970 World Cup, reviewing the 72 internationals which I personally directed between 1965 and 1980, I have to say that the England World Cup team of 1970 was the greatest of them all, and Bobby Charlton and Gordon Banks were two of the greatest players to wear the English shirt.

At the Jalisco Stadium, Guadalajara, we occupied the same commentary position for every match, ITV likewise, except that they were immediately in front of us and down a step. We were not aware of them (and vice versa) until they stood up. In '70, at the Mexico World Cup, because ITV had commentator Brian Moore and summariser Billy Wright, former England captain, at the commentary position, young Mexicans would continually bring around cups of Coca-Cola. That was a nightmare for me. Coleman would always put his on top of the monitor, a very precarious position, so I would automatically lean over and place his Coca-Cola on the safer, more stable, table. This went on time after time, match after match. It was the England/Brazil match, one of the finest matches I had ever seen. The little Mexican had just delivered his cups of Coca-Cola when Brazil scored; Coleman thumped the table at the same time. The Coca-Cola disappeared over the front of the table, the contents pouring completely over the heads of those unfortunate enough to be in front of us. Just as the hullabaloo was dying down, slowly, ever so slowly, a head appeared. It belonged to the most capped and famous footballer in England, one Billy Wright. Coca-Cola streamed through his blond curly hair, down over his eyes and nose, down around his ears, and into his once-clean white shirt. The apparition spoke: 'I know the BBC don't like ITV, but don't you think this is carrying it too far!'

In the final Brazil turned on their magic to beat Italy 4–1, and I was there to see the great Pele not only score a goal but play and score in his last World Cup match.

The quarter finals of the 1972 European Championship presented a few problems. England versus West Germany. We lost the first leg played at Wembley 3–1. The second leg was due to be played in the Olympic Stadium, West Berlin, on a Saturday. There was only one match that could be the 'match of the day' and that was the international. After 48 hours of frantic phone calls I came up with the following answer. The match, introduction and linking would be recorded to London. The team would number 8: Commentator (Coleman), two 'experts' (Joe Mercer and Don Revie), (Jonathan Martin), Producer (myself), Assistant Producer (Jimmy Dumighan), Ronnie Noble and a former Editor of Sports Department. I hired a DH 125 Jet to take off from and return to Luton. Its journey time was just over the hour. Cheaper than two nights' accommodation for 7/8 people in a Berlin Hotel. All technical facilities were booked, Berlin studio and two cars. I planned for everything. Or so I thought. That's when things started going downhill.

In front of a packed Olympic Stadium England played a pretty awful game to draw with West Germany nil-nil. England were out of the European Championship. But there were no mistakes with our commentary team of David, Joe and Don, who then recorded to London links, interviews and comments and by eight o'clock all had been received in London. Our job was finished. The cars took us to the Hilton Hotel where we refreshed and enjoyed a good strong drink. I had reserved a table for eight for dinner in the Hilton's executive Chandelier Restaurant – *the* place to dine on a Saturday evening, which was what Herr Willy Brandt, Chancellor of West Germany, always did with his wife and three daughters. At about nine o'clock we were shown to our table. We ordered and tucked into some wonderful German wine. Starters came and were devoured and then, eventually, the main course. We were all tucking in when one of the immaculately dressed flunkeys appeared with a very ornate, white eighteenth-century-style telephone.

'A call from BBC London,' spoke the flunkey. Jonathan Martin, the studio director of *M.O.T.D.*, jumped up practically throwing his dinner off the table and shouted, 'Here. Here. Here!' The phone was passed to him. What transpired for the next few minutes still brings tears to my eyes.

'Hello, London. Jonathan Martin here.' Pause. 'Hello, London. Can you hear me?' Pause. These two sentences were repeated several times but with ever increasing volume. He had started seated but after about the eighth try he was standing, with one knee on the huge round table, screaming at the top of his voice, 'Hello, London.'

The restaurant had fallen silent. The string trio in the corner had stopped playing. Herr Willy Brandt and his family, seated at the next table, were horror struck. Coleman, who had attempted to carry on eating his beautifully cooked steak, finally slammed down his knife and fork, leant forward and said, 'Jonathan. You're *******shouting into the ear-piece.'

By the time the rest of us stopped laughing, our dinner was cold.

West Germany, 1974. A great World Cup, great football. But, without doubt, the incident that took the biscuit involved a well-known team after they were eliminated at the end of the first round. Throughout their stay they had been followed, harassed, pestered by autograph hunters, one of their number in particular. Now, these fanatical collectors are not necessarily fifteen or sixteen years old. One particular German fanatic was about thirty and supported this team from overseas with the fervour of a big-game hunter.

His knowledge of his idols was minutely detailed. He was no Adonis, standing about five feet seven, with thin, wispy-to-balding fair hair, but he was also never alone – he always had in tow his wife, a smashing German blonde with a voluptuous figure, always dressed in a tight-fitting sweater that emphasised her large, bra-less breasts. When the first player appeared outside the team hotel in the morning this couple would be there; when the last of the players disappeared at night, they were there. And the same at the stadium training ground, where he became instantly animated at the sight of a player while she remained aloof, silent, just standing there, watching, as if waiting for something.

140

The team were eliminated, as I have said, at the end of the first round. Nevertheless, a celebration dinner and end-of-term party took place at the hotel. Someone took pity on this couple, who were soon seated at the same table as eight or nine of the players, their idols.

For five or six weeks these sportsmen had abstained from the many things which all good sportsmen abstain from at certain times. So, whilst four of the team enthralled our German fanatic with autographs, photographs and team souvenirs, the remaining five took his wife for a little walk ... upstairs... Sixty minutes later the five international players reappeared, a little bleary-eyed, tired, but contented-looking. They were followed by an even more ravishing, buoyant, nipples-projecting, sprightly German Frau. She pecked her husband lightly on the cheek, who, I'm sure, had not noticed her absence, and picking up a large tankard of lager proceeded to down it in one. Thirsty work.

Germany won the World Cup that year in more ways than one!

My memories of the 1978 Argentinian World Cup are many.

Our famous personality urgently telephoned from his hotel room for the interpreter. This was urgent. Top priority. It took 20 frantic minutes to rush the interpreter from the press centre to our personality's room. It had to be at the very least the translation from Spanish into English of the Polish team's playing formation. But no. It turned out to be, 'How the hell do you order cannelloni in Spanish?'

Room 601 in the Gran Hotel Dora was the BBC's office. A room with an en-suite bathroom. Eighteen people and 24-hour circuits and desks can make a room like this seem crowded and noisy. Our radio comrades were also using the sound circuit every day for reporting live, or for recording into Radios 1, 2, 3 and 4, and we couldn't all work in the same place at the same time. Therefore, we decided to build a sound studio in the bathroom. Curtains were taken down and hung over the shower rail; wires were extended into the bathroom, and on 1st June 1978 one had the sight of Denis Law sitting on the edge of the bath and Brian Butler sitting on the toilet (smoking his pipe, of course), both wearing headphones: 'This is Brian Butler speaking to you from a sunny, excited Córdoba...'

One of the most important things in Argentina was the 'Journalist League'. It was formed by the British media, written and electronic, based in Córdoba, to assess progress with the beautiful women of Argentina. A private dinner party warranted one point, coffees and brandies at her home, two points, etc. A member of the BBC team, I regret to inform you, was bottom of the league, but, after a pre-World Cup reception to thank our friends in Argentina television in advance for their hospitality, Mr X was seen to depart with a beautiful brunette on his arm. 'I'll get off the bottom of the league tonight.'

'Where do you live, my dear?' he said to his lady-friend.

'Alta Gracia.' (45 kilometres south of Córdoba.)

'Ah well, who cares? Taxi!'

Unfortunately, our BBC colleague had had a busy day and fell asleep in the car, waking up when the taxi got back to his hotel, minus his lady-friend, who had hopped out at Alta Gracia. Cost? 20,000 pesos. He was still minus seven points in the league when he left Argentina 28 days later!

Argentina, and Buenos Aires in particular, were still talking about the senior BBC executive's arrival at the capital city's airport with a fair amount of excess baggage, including a heavy video-cassette recorder. As the luggage began to appear on the airport conveyor belt, the first package was the BBC's VCR. Our executive reached for it, but being British (Welsh) and having played a bit of rugby in his day he refused to let go, and as it weighed 100 lb or more he was pulled onto the conveyor belt. Still gripping his parcel, he went slowly through the leather apron, out towards the tarmac, past bemused Argentinian baggage porters and guards, and then back again into the baggage-collection hall and the three BBC staff waiting to greet their chief. 'Give me a hand, boyo, it's a bit heavy,' says an unruffled Cliff Morgan.

In Córdoba it didn't take our technicians long to sort out the bargain spots, and they found one, a shop, just off the main square. It sold leather and suede jackets and jerkins at a fantastically cheap price. Back home in London one would pay three times the price. All of us were very impressed and later on, when we had time, we would get around to buying something in leather or suede. But for the time being we were busy. Well, most of us were, although not so a certain commentator. One day, back at our hotel, he suddenly let everyone know that we could buy our leather goods from a new source – himself. He had bought every jacket and jerkin in the shop. Emptied it completely. Of course, the goods were not quite as cheap as they had been when we had seen them in the shop a few days earlier!

One evening in a Córdoba restaurant, two ITV lads, well-known names in TV soccer, were sitting having a meal. In walked a beautiful Argentinian woman, escorted by a huge 6ft 4in Argentinian male. The two ITV Romeos sat drooling and mouthing romantic platitudes, much to the amusement of the damsel, but to the annoyance of her escort. When our two heroes went and sat at the same table, uninvited, the gigantic Argentinian was livid. A fight surely had to materialise. But no, half an hour later the four were laughing together and were about to set off to a club escorted by the South American beauty.

When they got to the club they sensed something was different. All the women were in one group, and the men were in another. An hour later the truth dawned on the two ITV lads. The giant Argentinian man of men turned out to be homosexual. The beautiful Argentinian woman was a lesbian.

It was one of *those* World Cups for ITV.

Spain 1982. Jimmy Hill was in a very strong position within the Beeb at that time and had insisted on introducing and being in vision for ALL our World Cup programmes, both in London and Spain. This entailed flying him backwards and forwards, sometimes by private jet, so that he could appear on screen at the start of every programme. I protested but the bosses agreed. Thus expensive but highly organised flights were arranged until the fatal occasion when he arrived at Valencia airport without his passport. 'But everyone knows me, I'm Jimmy Hill.' Unfortunately, the armed immigration at the Spanish airport of Valencia had not heard of one Señor James Hill. His passport had been left on a desk at TV Centre. A young production assistant, desperately needed in London, was designated to fly at once to Valencia with Jimmy's passport; from then onwards Jimmy was to be accompanied at all times by his young minder. Having been released by Spanish Immigration, Jimmy went striding off, but he did not get to the stadium in time to introduce the programme.

Now, I may not have mentioned that, no matter how large a team we had we were all on a daily allowance. Our hotel and air fares would be paid, but for our meals, laundry, etc., we had an

Jimmy Hill and Bobby Robson, World Cup 1982.

allowance, agreed with management, i.e. the allowances office and the unions. I had made several visits to Spain during the two-year build-up and had come to the conclusion that £33 per day would leave everyone very comfortably financially provisioned. Of course the unions objected. It didn't help that one of our senior engineers working in Spain happened to be the chairman of the union, and he, of course, wanted to flex his muscles. The allowance officers got scared – administrators are normally frightened of the unions – and they came up with what to them seemed a brilliant suggestion. Over the Easter break (administrators always got a long Easter break, i.e. from Thursday evening until the following Tuesday morning) the allowances department would send four members of their department to stay at the four main areas that we, the BBC World Cup team, would be occupying: staying in our booked hotels, eating locally, and generally spending what we would spend. The only exception to this was that we were normally so damned busy we never had time to *spend*. So at about 5 on that Thursday evening four members of the allowances department flew off to their

144

destinations in Spain – Madrid, Bilbao, Valencia and Málaga – where they stayed until the Tuesday after Easter. For the remainder of that week these four were locked in private discussion with their boss, the Head of Allowances, until at 4 o'clock on the Friday the allowances officer rang to tell me, after a long preamble concerning the magnificent fortitude of his staff, 'so I have informed the unions, who have agreed, of course, that the daily allowance for staff working in Spain during the World Cup will be £33'. Which was exactly the figure I had suggested to them some three months earlier! About two months after this matter had been settled, and nearly forgotten (except by myself, as you can tell), I received a charge to my World Cup budget of £2,900 for five nights. But it wasn't four persons, it was eight. Each member of staff had been accompanied by their spouse or partner. 'I thought a second opinion would be valuable,' said the Head of Allowances when I rang him to query the large bill!

Talking of World Cup budgets, throughout the '80s, whilst working on these major overseas big-budget programmes, planners, controllers, the Director-General, always expected me to submit an estimated programme budget at least eighteen months in advance; in other words, long before we knew which countries would qualify for the World Cup, which in turn would decide the number of staff working on the project, the cost of hotels, allowances, etc. And yet one was expected to come in, 20 months later, at least ten per cent under one's crystal-ball-gazing estimate.

By October 1981, we knew that Northern Ireland, Scotland and England had reached the final rounds of the 82 World Cup. It was pretty certain that they would each be located within a different part of Spain and it was therefore essential to have electronic facilities to interview managers and players of that particular team. Vision and sound lines in Spain in 1982 were not readily to hand. A day's notice, yes, but not within the hour. So we took as part of our technical equipment a mobile satellite dish, but this was not one of your 21st-century 2-foot dishes that can transmit from anywhere in the world.

Our 1982 mobile satellite dish was – 22 feet in diameter!

It looked quite unusual to see this 2-ton object being trundled through quaint Spanish villages. Masses of paperwork had to be filled in. Certain bribes to government officials, of both countries. Our dish was one of a pair, the other having been confiscated by

M.O.D. for use in the Falklands war. Officials within Whitehall just could not find the location of our dish to transport that also to the Falklands war.

We used it extensively throughout Spain and were able to get scoop after scoop over our competitor, ITV.

Though we were a team, there is always someone who wants more than anyone else. In Spain we had our reporter/commentator from Argentina, you know, from the leather-jacket-shop-in-Córdoba episode. He had been in Spain for 14 days, and we were 10 days into the World Cup. He came in one day with a sheaf of paper representing his expenses for 'entertaining football contacts'. Broken down this meant 14 days of breakfasts, 14 days of lunches and 14 days of dinners, the restaurant being sometimes 200 miles away from his hotel. You always get one greedy so and so on any team.

The 1982 Spanish World Cup promised to be the biggest in every sense of the word. For the first time 24 teams were playing, at 14 different grounds. We sent five commentators to cover the matches, but our Head of Sport decided that John Motson should commentate on all the major matches, even though Barry Davies was just as competent as Motson. The only way to get Motson, and therefore the other commentators, around from one venue to another was by private plane, one that could take off whenever the commentator had reached the airstrip after his match. I hired a plane and crew from England, but to meet Spanish civil aviation regulations the company flying the plane had to own its own plane. So for the sum of £25,000 the BBC, via our solicitor, bought the plane. Officially, we were the owners one day before the World Cup began until one day after the World Cup had finished. The enterprise was 100 per cent successful. Well, very nearly.

England were playing in the Bilbao group, against France, Czechoslovakia and Kuwait. The first match was against France in Bilbao on the 16th June. For weeks the British press had been forecasting a bloodbath at Bilbao the day that England and France played, which would be even worse if England lost. England won 3–1. Bilbao was not burnt down, French supporters were not automatically beaten up by British hooligans, but instead that evening saw the British supporters supping and drinking with the French locals, everyone arm in arm. The British press did not have a story. They, several of them, were commiserating with each other at a well-known Bilbao hostelry when in walked four or five BBC

146

fellows. They knew the press boys and very soon they were all exchanging stories about the World Cup, etc. Rounds of drinks had been exchanged when a certain member of the BBC production staff (he is now a senior producer in the sports department) mentioned the BBC plane.

'What BBC plane?' asked one of the reporters. 'Oh, didn't you know, we had our own plane,' says our man. 'Sure, I'll have another drink.' And so the conversation and the buying of drinks for our BBC person went on for another hour, particularly by journalists from the *Mirror*, the *Sun* and the *Star*. Those three journalists left the bar at about 8.30 p.m., much to the disappointment of the only remaining BBC person, who by now was well and truly sloshed. I, in Madrid, was unaware of all this, until the following morning at about 9 o'clock, when I arrived at our office complex at the international broadcasting centre. The English newspapers were awaiting me on my desk, flown in by BA. I flipped through them and was suddenly frozen by the headline in the *Daily Mirror*: 'LUXURY BBC PLANE FLIES COMMENTATORS AROUND SPAIN'. What followed was utter gibberish about the luxuries and the purpose of the plane. I moved the paper as I was reading and caught the headline of the *Sun*: 'MOTSON HAS OWN LUXURY PLANE IN SPAIN'. More gibberish. Then the *Star*: 'BBC SPEND LICENCE MONEY ON LUXURY PLANE'. More lies under the banner headline.

Just then the phone rang. 'Mr Weeks, Chairman's Assistant, Mrs Melrose, here. I have a message from the Chairman. May I read it to you?' I grunted my agreement, my mind still on the newspapers in front of me. 'The message from the Chairman, Mr Howard, reads: "You are to catch the next plane back to England and return home. Your services are terminated. Someone from Administration will contact you Monday next."' I was speechless. 'I will teleprint this to you immediately, Mr Weeks', and down went the phone.

I sat there thunderstruck. Frozen. There was a rattle and banging outside. The door opened. It was Cliff. Cliff Morgan. 'Hello, boyo,' he shouts. Then, looking at my face, he said, 'What's wrong?', reading correctly that I had problems. I quickly told him. 'I've been fired.' Then the teleprinter started chuntering and there was my telephone message from the Chairman's Assistant, in print. 'Leave this to me, Weeksey,' said Cliff, and within minutes he was on the phone to the BBC's solicitor, a Mr Jennings. He, in turn, once Cliff had spelt it all out, got on to the Chairman, Mr George Howard, who was still in his office at Broadcasting House and indeed had been there when his assistant had spoken to me. He hadn't had the courage to do the dirty work himself. It seems that the solicitor spent 10 minutes on the phone to the Chairman. Then he came back, spoke to Cliff, then asked to speak to me. 'The Chairman says there must have been a misunderstanding by the press. You can stay in Spain.' No personal message or phone call, or personal apology. It's called man management. Two days after the World Cup we sold the plane back to its original owners – for a pound more than we paid for it!

One final little story. BBC News had a team of eight in Spain and, just like the British press, they had very few news stories. Everyone was enjoying themselves, and enjoyment does not make BBC news. So in a little pub not far from the Bernabeu Stadium in Madrid on the night of the 29th June, when England were due to play Germany in the second group stage, the BBC News team sent out a message to the English fans to meet in this pub about an hour and a half before the match. They had paid the owner to supply the English fans with whatever they wanted to drink, about one hundred and fifty pounds' worth to be exact. They then informed the local police of this gathering. The police came in their dozens, at least half a dozen mounted, then the three news cameras were positioned, one even shooting between the legs of the horse – very artistic.

With about 45 minutes to go before the match, the English fans, all of whom had tickets, started to file out of the pub. As they did so, the Spanish police hit them over the head, shoulders, legs, and arms with their long batons, then pushed them, punched them, tripped them. The supporters were not drunk. Happy, yes. But not drunk. That evening not one of those 50 or 60 English fans escaped without a bruise; some were really knocked about, especially some of the girls. Fellows are used to sidestepping, ducking, but not girls. So the BBC's three newsreel cameras got some sensational shots of the so-called English hooligans, staggering around under horses' hooves, not from drink, as the later commentary had it, but really from the blows of the police batons. Those that attempted to fight back, or rather defend their girlfriends, were promptly arrested, about 10 in total. Later that evening, just after the transmission of the goalless draw between Germany and England, a beautifully shot

148

and edited 4-minute story went out from the Madrid international broadcasting centre to TV Centre, London, with an appropriate commentary, once again depicting the downfall of the English soccer hooligan. And really those 60 youngsters were just a happy, harmless bunch of soccer enthusiasts – but not by the time the BBC News had finished setting them up.

One shouldn't always believe what one sees on TV news.

So it's back to Mexico for the 1986 World Cup. Sure, we hired a small plane to get our commentary teams around. The *Mirror*, the *Sun* and the *Star* continuously cadged a lift. Friendly people, marvellous stadiums and matches, but in spite of the usual television problems the question that had to be answered occurred nine months earlier.

19th September 1985. I had been planning this World Cup for a couple of years. England, Scotland and Northern Ireland had just qualified. My budget had been agreed at £4 million and I had already spent $1\frac{1}{4}$ million on hotel deposits, satellite booking, office space, etc. This was going to be a big operation. It was mid-afternoon when an urgent teleprint message arrived on my desk:

> Mexico City Earthquake. At ten past seven this morning an eleven-minute holocaust struck the City of Mexico. Between ten and fifteen thousand were reported killed. No hotels were standing. Five square miles of devastation has reduced the city to rubble. Rumour after rumour is spilling from the city...

I tried phoning, but to no avail. I read every report I could get my hands on, then, two days after the disaster, Bill Cotton, the Managing Director of BBC Television, rang me. 'Have you got any direct contact with Mexico?' 'Nothing,' I replied. 'How much have you spent so far on the Mexico World Cup?' I replied, 'About $1\frac{1}{2}$ million.' 'Well, get over there as fast as you can and let us know whether we are going to lose our money.' I was on a plane the following day, arriving in Mexico City four days after the earthquake had devastated the place – and a devastated place it was.

Demolition work had begun in earnest and at every damaged site huge cranes, bulldozers, lorries and thousands of people were working round the clock under arc lamps, clambering over the rubble and digging with everything, including their bare hands. The water supplies were in a bad way; in many parts of the city sewage was seeping into the water supply. Everyone was being ordered to boil water before using it. Huge areas of the city looked as if giant waves had hit the road, and some pavements were raised by as much as 10 feet. Throughout my stay in Mexico City there was this familiar smell – one of decay, rotting flesh, soot and dust everywhere. For me it was like turning back the clock forty-odd years to London in 1943. After the clean-up Mexico City would look like London in 1945.

Televisa, the major broadcasting network in Mexico City, was one of the victims of the disaster. Its 380-foot masts had collapsed, taking with them three transmitters, a major studio where the 'Breakfast Programme' had been in full swing ... and the canteen. More than one hundred staff of Televisa were reported dead or missing. I was actually walking around Televisa five days after the earthquake had struck; on one side the many teams of workers were digging away looking for the dead or injured, whilst on the opposite side of the large area the bulldozers were working side by side filling in the craters and attempting to put the site back to how it was, actually filling in the holes and covering up and burying bodies that lay underneath. Life was, and still is, cheap in Mexico.

I visited the stadiums, particularly the major stadium for the World Cup, the famous Aztec Stadium. I walked all around this gigantic place, both inside and outside; there were cracks running right from the top to the very bottom, cracks that were so wide I could actually place my arm inside. I met and spoke to many members of the World Cup organising committee. All were full of optimism; a few hold-ups, but that was all. As I left the city five days later, eight days after the earthquake, many hundreds were still queuing for water and food. I quickly compiled a four-page report for Bill Cotton, finishing with the following:

There must be question marks over the large number of unsafe buildings in the capital and over the possibility of sewage creeping into the water supply. It is essential we take a BBC doctor. The demolition and scarred sites will look awful by next May, but London was not exactly a pretty site for the 1948 Olympics. Morally, the World Cup should not take place in Mexico. Technically, it will require a miracle. Financially, it will take place. We should cover it fully.

150

I was to return to Mexico in December in time for the draw. The roads leading to the stadiums were now all in perfect order. Huge scars were boarded up, not visible to the tourist. Cracks in stadium walls had all been repaired, and even the international centre seemed to be nearing completion, though admittance to technical areas such as the international control room was not possible for some apparently simple reason. Charges for broadcasting facilities were gigantic, so one was entitled to believe that all was in order for the broadcasting of the Mexico World Cup.

This was not so. Behind the scenes poverty, hunger and homelessness had increased tenfold. One felt ashamed to eat in smart restaurants and book accommodation for June and July in five-star hotels.

I returned to Mexico in May.

I was to find out later that all work on the broadcasting facilities had come to a complete standstill for three months. All efforts in Mexico were directed to putting the country back to working normally as soon as possible. There was not enough time to put together the world's broadcasting facilities, but they desperately needed the money that would be coming in from the world's broadcasters.

Everything had to be paid for in advance. Indeed, several networks, including the BBC, were not allowed into their offices until desks, chairs and even coat stands had been paid for in advance.

The source of the broadcasting disaster was simple. The Mexicans, after clearing up following the earthquake, were so busy taking and making money they forgot to test the equipment at commentary positions at the various stadiums. At the Aztec Stadium in Mexico City for the opening ceremony and first match of the 1986 World Cup, Italy v. Bulgaria, 130 commentary positions were requested and paid for in advance by the world's broadcasters.

Only 64 worked. But worse was still to come.

On the second day, 1st June, at the Jalisco Stadium, Guadalajara, for the Brazil v. Spain match, 69 commentary positions were booked and paid for; one worked – TV Globo, Brazil. John Motson did our commentary from Guadalajara to Television Centre, Wood Lane, West London on an ordinary telephone.

And so this farcical situation went on and on for five horrendous

151

days. There were some commentators who had travelled thousands of miles to sit in a commentary position for match after match only for their commentary not even to leave the stadium. CBC of Canada, for instance, did commentary on eight matches before finally being successful on the ninth match, Portugal v. England.

From day two I had our engineers on duty from 5.30 a.m. onwards every day, not only at the international broadcasting centre, but also at the stadiums. This way we screamed, nagged, bullied, pleaded with any and, at times, all the Mexican engineers, who, as we were the first on the spot, at least gave us first attention ... and some of our circuits worked. We definitely came off better than ITV, who generally did not come on duty until 8 or 8.30 a.m. each morning; consequently, they were way down in the pecking order. By 6th June the situation had improved, but not before the whole world had complained and objected to their respective governments.

It was from day five, when the broadcasting of the Mexican World Cup was turning into one of the biggest media fiascos of all time, that we took the law into our own hands. We had been leaving the objections to our so-called leaders in the EBU, the European Broadcasting Union, who were supposed to represent all their members. They were spineless, always playing politics and thinking of themselves. Eight very senior, but above all, experienced, engineers formed a group comprising one from the BBC, one from ITV and then one each German, Swedish, Finnish, Argentinian, French and Australian television. They pushed, barged, cajoled, shouted their way into the international control room, some receiving very painful digs in the body from the bayoneted rifles of the security guards. That was where the problem lay, in the central control room. It was the key link-up point of the whole broadcasting centre; there was wire going everywhere except into the right junction boxes. These eight international engineers, assisted now by the half a dozen Mexican engineers, locked themselves into the international control room and finally came out again 36 hours later, with everything linked up to and from its correct destination. Three months' technical work had been lost following the earthquake and no matter how hard the Mexican engineers worked they just could not catch up on all the backlog. This was where the trouble lay for those first five days of broadcasting, and it very nearly led to the biggest broadcasting flop of all time.

The 1986 World Cup cost the BBC £4 million. Of course domestic problems occurred, in addition to the traumatic technical shambles, like one of our reporters deciding that he did not like flying. He left the BBC soon afterwards to form his own religion! Another was a certain person threatening to return home every other day unless he appeared in vision on everything. He now works for Sky. Another wanted his room changed six or seven times. In short, the usual temperamental problems.

It was one of our personalities who, to butter up the players and officials, encouraged the members of the England team to use the BBC direct-line phone in our office to speak to their wives or girlfriends at home. The Scottish team got to hear of this and of course they had to have the same facility. This 'favour' by our 'personality' cost us £20,000 in extra telephone calls. (Yes, it was the same man who first appears in chapter six.)

We had our own plane again, and what a blessing it was. The internal Mexican airlines are some of the worst in the world; 50 per cent of flights do not take off and the remainder fly late. So for an outlay of $30,000 we were completely independent.

We also took our own medical officer, Dr John Newman. An unusual, but not a surprising move after having been told of the sewers being cracked in the September earthquake, their contents leaking into the drinking water, and of Montezuma's revenge, the gastric stomach ailment which is the most violent form of dysentery. In this regard, each member of the team had a note from me awaiting them when they arrived in our hotel, it included the following:

GENERAL PRECAUTIONS FOR BBC TRAVELLERS IN MEXICO
Do *not* eat raw vegetables or fruits *unless* they can be peeled and you peel them yourself.
Avoid lettuce and other green leafy vegetables.
Do *not* eat raw or rare meat or fish.
Avoid milky/dairy products, e.g. ice cream and soft cheeses.
Avoid eating food purchased from street vendors.
Eat well-cooked foods which are still hot.
A useful tip is to inspect restaurant toilet facilities. If they are in poor repair, unkempt and dirty, you may reasonably assume that the kitchen's workers' loos are worse, indicating inadequate hygienic practices at the restaurant.

OTHER PRECAUTIONS
Avoid bottled non-carbonated, i.e. 'still', water.
Avoid drinking the bathroom tap water.
Avoid ice in all drinks.

I always base my advice on hard fact. One morning I just couldn't get to sleep. I thought I would go for a walk around the block. It was about 4.30 a.m., and the sun was just rising. A large lorry came around a corner at the back of our hotel and stopped. A couple of fellows in the back then pushed and dragged a huge lump of ice onto the pavement. It smashed to the ground. It was about five foot square. The lorry roared off into the distance. Just then a large lurcher-type dog came strolling up, sniffed the ice, and peed right onto it. The ice was then broken up and dragged into the hotel, but not before a few more of our lurcher's four-legged friends had paid a call! From then onwards I always made sure, when in Mexico, I never had ice in my drink.

Approximately one-third of our team were hypochondriacs, and I told everyone to use bottled water only to clean their teeth. Still, when 25 per cent of our team started going sick Dr John came into his own and did a magnificent job.

It was around 7th June, just as our technical problems were getting sorted when, after an exceptionally heavy storm, the basement of the international broadcasting centre slowly started to fill with water. Our complex of offices and studios happened to be alongside the power room, across the corridor from the international control room, and literally surrounded by high-voltage equipment, so when members of the Mexican Army started using squeegees to push back the water I knew exactly how King Canute must have felt. I'm still here, so obviously it stopped raining, but not until the water was gently lapping one inch from the main fuse box!

I was very worried about the money situation in Mexico, with the peso/dollar exchange rate going like a yo-yo. So I elected to open a bank account in San Antonio, just over the US border, in Texas. The day after our arrival in Mexico, Lesley Morris, my assistant, and I took a trip up to San Antonio, collected all our cheque-books, and, heart in mouth, $100,000 in currency in a briefcase. One could not get dollar currency in Mexico and, whether I liked it or not, players and officials do like to be paid in cash and would not accept pesos, only dollars So we flew back into

154

Mexico, moved up to customs to be asked, 'Señor, any pills, and sugar, any medicines?'

'No,' I replied calmly, and we walked through customs with $100,000 in the briefcase; the limit was $1,000. What the hell, it's only a job of work, even if one is not just an old-fashioned television producer, but a financial genius, a catering manager, a travel agent, a nurse, or certainly a crook.

So do you still think these trips are simple, straightforward and glamorous?

All in all, we had in Mexico, judging by my 35 years' experience of these overseas jobs, the finest BBC team I can recall. There is nothing like a crisis to close ranks and bind a team together.

Chapter Ten

Lap of Honour

In the 1930s an ECHO wireless set brought to me not only the big fights but the Cup Finals, especially the ones featuring Preston North End, Sunderland, or Arsenal. To me Cup Final Day was special, an occasion. And when I produced for television 16 Cup Finals between 1966 and 1980 I still attempted to treat Cup Final Day as a special occasion.

In 1966 for the Everton/Sheffield Wednesday match I did not realise until 2.15 p.m., when the crowd were singing to the military bands, how emotional they became. And by 2.40, when the first note of *Abide with Me* was heard, it was easy to instruct one's close-up cameras to find a shot of 'an old boy, white haired, medals on his chest, singing his head off'. Often his tears would run down his face onto his ribbons. There weren't many dry eyes sitting in front of 'the box' when I transmitted that shot. For those 34–40 minutes we concentrated on the emotions of the day and by the time the teams came walking out of the players' tunnel onto the pitch at 2.45 we had our audience riveted to the screen.

We had six cameras at Wembley in '66; by 1980 that had grown to 15: 2 or 3 cameras were outside the stadium, some along Wembley Way getting the atmosphere of the arriving fans, the colour, the noise, the atmosphere, even interviewing 'the famous': the ministers, the film stars and sportsmen, on the steps of the VIP Enclosure. We also had cameras in the two respective team hotels and on the coaches bringing the teams to Wembley. With the right sort of weather, the GoodYear Airship could show the viewer not only the stadium, but all the approaching roads – used occasionally it was very effective. And with all this in colour, it was some transmission.

Which brings me to the photograph at the end of the chapter, which was taken in April 1976 at Leicester City Football Club, who that day were playing Manchester United. Leicester won 2–1 but the bonus for the 30 people in that photo was that Manchester United were, the following week, Saturday May 1st, playing Second Division Southampton in the FA Cup Final at Wembley. And by featuring the Manchester club in *Match of the Day* it gave everyone just another 'dress rehearsal'. This was the fourth time this crew had televised United that month. With Southampton they had covered one match but visited them in training twice and had sat and talked to them a week earlier. Barry Davies was our commentator at Leicester but at Wembley he would be carrying out interviews on the pitch and elsewhere and David Coleman would be our commentator for the '76 Cup Final.

Camera and sound had seen both teams in action, studied recordings, attended training sessions, met and talked to the players after training, even carried postcard photos of the teams. I made sure that most of the crew stayed at the Wembley hotel the night before. Over dinner I thought they seemed very relaxed and composed, they had a job to do and knew how to do it. Looking at that photo of all 29 I really couldn't fault anyone.

The six Vision Engineers sitting in the centre of the control van, matching the colours of each camera: the reds, the blues, the yellows; the hands flitting over the controls for every second of the five-hour transmission. Perfect.

Camera One. The Master Camera, Senior Cameraman Teddy Cocks due to retire in about a year, his coverage was just poetic, seeing the forward line sweep up the pitch zooming in on the goalmouth. An artist using his brushes with skill.

Camera Two – Phil Jones. Hovering for the close-up action, the tackle, the save,

Camera Three – Keith Williams. Close-ups when the ball is dead, the team-bench.

Camera Four – Barry Chaston. The 'personality' camera, positioned ten feet from the touch-line, Barry operating a powerful zoom-lens positioned in a three-foot trench. He was so fast that day, so steady, so reliable, so sure.

Cameras Five and Six, each positioned immediately behind a goal and operated by John Pilblad and Alan Hayward. To see the penalty box incidents in slow-motion from their low camera position behind the goals was 'Hollywood' coverage at its best.

Sound, besides numerous commentary and interview microphones, had eighteen effects mics dotted around the pitch and slung high in the roof over the crowd. Keith Harlow's hands were moving over the sound desk from 2 o'clock until 5.15, providing the complete backcloth to the pictures.

I had two Team Liaison chaps in the stadium that day, Jimmy Dumighan and Bill Platts, who never stopped running. It was their job to keep in touch with the teams in the dressing room, on the pitch, collect players for interviews, generally passing all information to the commentator. Great to rely on these two.

The same must be said about the commentator. That day David Coleman used every piece of broadcasting technique and knowledge he had gained over 25 years, timing to name the player just as the camera had focused and I had 'punched' up the shot.

In my own mind I know why we were so dammed brilliant that day. On the ball! It was the 'warm-up'. Frank Bough handed over to David Coleman just after 2 p.m. Fifteen minutes earlier than planned, he said he misheard instructions from TV Centre. Nevertheless his mistake was our gain. The crowd had started to 'warm-up' and on that particular Saturday no one 'warmed-up' louder than the 63,000 fans from Lancashire and Hampshire. We had 50 minutes to fill, to cover, to present the atmosphere within the stadium before the players entered the 'field of play'. For just a few seconds I thought we had taken on too much, but all trepidation disappeared with, 'All Right, Big Al. Let's show them. I'll follow your shots.' David's words did it. Not under any pressure we really milked the atmosphere. The respective groups of fans behind each goal were in magnificent voice and waved their colours in time with the singing. A sea of colour from both ends. When the famous *Abide with Me* was reached my cameras 2 and 3 seemed to find the 'old-soldiers-with-white-hair-and-war-ribbons' perfectly and I guarantee there were not many dry eyes in the drawing rooms at 2.45, when the teams came out of the tunnel on the last notes of the famous hymn. All this gave us a terrific 'warm-up'; settled our nerves and meant that we covered the match with great confidence. We never missed a trick.

The national newspapers had given Southampton, who were appearing at Wembley for the first time, no chance whatsoever. And though Manchester United had the better footballers, Southampton were so relaxed and their tactics, designed by brilliant

159

BBC outside broadcast producer Alec Weeks receiving from HRH Princess Anne the award for the Best Outside Broadcast of 1976, The FA Cup Final.

© Michael J. Barrett

manager Lawrie McMenemy, frustrated and contained the Lancashire side enough for Bobby Stokes to put the ball past Alex Stepney seven minutes from the final whistle and win for Southampton their first major trophy.

Southampton performed like masters that day and so did our Outside Broadcast crew. Every one of them.

From 2 o'clock, the time when we 'took over', I wasn't aware of ITV presence at any time whatsoever. If there was any time in my broadcasting career that I knew our coverage had been better than 'the opposition' it was then. Wembley, 1976 Cup Final. Audience figures: BBC 15 million, ITV 7 million.

Nearly a year later, in April 1977 at the BAFTA Awards (British Academy Film and Television Arts) at the newly completed Wembley Arena I received from Her Royal Highness, Princess Anne, The President of BAFTA, the Trophy for the Best Outside Broadcast of the Year – The 1976 FA Cup Final, Manchester United v Southampton. The BAFTA awards that year were televised live by the BBC. The

160

Senior Cameraman of the Unit transmitting the awards was one Barry Chaston, one of the heroes. The first telegram I was to receive the following day was from Southampton's Lawrie McMenemy, the manager of that great team, which was exactly what I had on May 1st, 1976 – A Great Team.

The BBC team: Back row (left to right): Mac Eaglen, rigger; Ron Suckling, caption artist; 'Jack Dempsey', rigger; Dick Newell, rigger; John Duffin, rigger; Eddie Hagger, rigger; Ron Lloyd, Stan Gene, radio links; Bill Platts, team liaison.
Middle row: Neville Alcock, stage manager; Julia Anderson, producer's assistant; Mike Daymon, radio links; Chris Neale, Chris Williams, vision engineers; Mike Jennings, senior vision engineer; Barry Davies, commentator; Ian Dow, Gerry Champion, Richard Hipkin, vision engineers; Keith Harlow, Senior sound engineer; Roger Ball, Geoff Kindon, sound engineers.
Front row: Keith Williams, Phil Jones, John Pilblad, Alan Hayward, Barry Chaston, Teddy Cocks, cameramen. Foreground: Alec Weeks, producer.

Chapter Eleven

The Olympic Oath:
'It is not the winning but the taking part'
(You must be joking!)

Innsbruck, 1964. The Winter Olympics. Britain was one of 36 competing countries with, for those days, a sizeable team of 50. These were the days when the sports department tried to do these big events on a shoestring. Cost-saving was high up on the list, and one of the budget-reducing ideas was room sharing. With a great act of wisdom for which the BBC is famous, I was paired with David Coleman. Two more opposite individuals one could not have found. Neither of us liked taking orders, being bullied, led, urged, etc. What was even worse was that our duties were completely opposite.

David was at the Winter Olympics to commentate on the opening and closing ceremonies, the two- and four-man bobs and the luge. I was there to direct the nightly 1½-hour *Olympic Round-up* programme which was transmitted about 10.30 each evening. David was working from about 5 a.m. until 3 p.m. In those days the bob runs were not electronically frozen; one had to rely on nature. Consequently, the bob and luge competitions started at 5 o'clock in the morning, so David was rising about 3.30 a.m., thus disturbing me. Finishing about midnight, I would come lumbering into the room at about 1 a.m., interrupting his night's sleep. It was chaotic, to say the least. Coleman would often try and get his own back; for instance, he would wait until I was practically stripped naked and standing in front of the washbasin (the Central Hotel, where we were boarded, was fairly old-fashioned and only had one bathroom on each floor, so strip washes were in order), then, unbeknown to

163

me, would press the bell for the chambermaid, who would come flying in. She would burst into fits of giggles, backed up with roars of laughter from Coleman, whilst I, starkers, attempted to cover my masculinity with a face towel! He caught me three times with this stunt. I tried to get my own back with a noisy, rude return from work at one o'clock in the morning, becoming noisier with each passing day. Then, towards the end of the Games, Coleman wanted a good night's sleep prior to the exhausting closing ceremony, so he bolted the door. One o'clock found me knocking timidly on the door. 'Come back in a couple of hours,' was the response. I went down to the bar and had a nightcap. Thirty minutes later I was knocking more aggressively. 'Come back in a couple of hours.' Another nightcap or two and, one hour on, it was approaching 3 a.m. Thumping the door brought the same comment. I took two steps back and hit the door – hard. Very, very hard. I was strong and fit in 1964. The door did not spring open – those Austrian locks and bolts were built to stay – but the whole frame, the uprights, the cross-beam and of course the door, just caved in, leaving the jagged brickwork and clouds and clouds of dust.

Through the dust appeared a startled Coleman, sitting up in bed. 'What the f—— hell have you done now, Alec?'

Even today, at the Central Hotel, Innsbruck, room 121, you can still see the newly bricked and cemented frame around the door.

A very interested observer throughout our Innsbruck operation was our Head of Sport, Bryan Cowgill. He was a brilliant operator, leader, and boss – ruthless, hard, but very fair. I knew he had missed the operational side very much indeed since being appointed Head of Sports Department in 1963 and becoming a desk-man. No matter how we tried we just could not get him to go to see some of the marvellous winter events. What was coming in from Austrian television, what our commentators were saying over these pictures and how we were treating, editing the events were the all-important thing to him, not socialising with foreign broadcasting dignitaries. So, every evening he could be found at the back of the gallery of our studio control room, where I was directing, groaning, complaining, grumbling, deep-sighing, and tut-tutting. Now, Innsbruck was fairly new to the world of international sport and world broadcasting; therefore, all facilities were stretched to the limits. The hotel's two-to-a-room we know about; banking, transport, eating, heating – you name it and Innsbruck were down to their last sovereign.

One evening, when we were halfway through our evening programme, the power went. There were no lights, and all equipment came to a groaning halt and shut down. This was not just in our studio, and not just confined to the broadcasting centre, but affected the whole of Innsbruck. I turned and glanced out of the control-room window, which had overlooked the sparkling lights of this Olympic City. Nothing. Complete darkness. Black as a cat.

A second. Two seconds. Then from the back of the control room came the screaming, gravelly, rasping voice of our Head of Sport.

'Alec. What the f—— hell have you done now?'

The two-man bob, an event taking place in the middle of the night. As I previously mentioned, there were no refrigerated bob runs in '64, so the thing was to catch the run when it was still practically frozen solid. There were a couple of Brits in the two-man event: an accountant, Tony Nash, and an army officer, Robin Dixon. The British sporting public hardly knew them and only a few did within the field of international winter sports. That was, until 19th February.

The red-hot favourites were the two Italian entries. One was the Olympic and World Champion, Carlos Zardini, the other the fastest team in the world that year, also Italian. The bob was, and still is, contested on aggregate time for four runs: two one day and two the following day. After the first run Nash and Dixon were lying third. After the second and final run of that day they were lying second, squeezed just between the two Italian bobs. The experts started talking of 'the good luck of the British team' etc. All the rest of us, the Brits in Innsbruck, were whispering and mumbling our thoughts, frightened that if we were heard it would bring misfortune upon the heads of Nash and Dixon.

On the second and final day, everyone was there by 5 a.m., and by 6 a.m. the competition had been postponed until the following day: it was too warm and the ice on the track was melting. That night it was cold. Very cold. Bloody cold. The track froze. By 5.20 a.m., Nash and Dixon had completed their third run. They flew; they were faster than the Italians, who were now just a split second in front. Come the fourth and final run, the experts still expected the Italians to put the British unknowns in their place. I don't know

165

what happened mentally to Zardini and his partner Bonagura, but they put in their slowest run, whereas Nash and Dixon put in their fastest run of the competition. When all the shouting, screaming, etc. had died, Nash and Dixon had won the gold medal by 12 hundredths of a second, only the fourth time a Brit had won a gold medal since the inception of the Winter Olympics in 1924.

Then the party started; before Nash and Dixon had even left their bob, champagne was being handed to them. Things like dope tests were still an unspoken topic. So their immediate teammates were followed by members of the British team, skaters, ski jumpers, all flooding to the bob, all with bottles of champagne. We had a live transmission slot into the *One O'clock News*. 'Sure,' slurred the two lads, 'Delighted.' The British press were also pleased that their Olympic Games reports had a British twist at last. They also produced bottles of champagne.

By the time Nash and Dixon arrived at the international broadcasting centre at 12 o'clock, one hour before we were due on the air, they were legless. Absolutely plastered. Up to the gills. What took place during the next hour was fascinating to our overseas colleagues. They were walked up and down the length of this pretty-long corridor. At each end they were stopped and given a large mug of warm sweet coffee. Buckets of it were fed down their throats. At different points on their route they were both sick, but by one o'clock they could look one straight in the eye and talk fairly normally, though their voices were slightly high-pitched. What a day. What's the penalty for being drunk in charge of a gold medal?

Having spent a considerable amount of my National Service in Japan, I was confident of being a member of the BBC's team for its transmissions of the Tokyo Olympics. But often the BBC's thinking is not logical. It was decided that with my knowledge of the Japanese lingo – I would be the ideal person to direct the studio. At Lime Grove, West London.

Disappointed, nevertheless I set about planning an effective but simple studio to accommodate compere Cliff Michelmore who, besides opening and closing the one-and-a-half-hour late-night programme, would also link us from event to event. All very straightforward and alongside me to ensure a first-class programme was editor Cliff Morgan, always a live-wire with a sense of humour, which he was going to need during those 17 days of the Olympics.

The EBU, the European Broadcasting Union, of which the BBC

was a very active member, had decided that from 10.30 p.m. to midnight the highlights of the day's events would be relayed to Europe via a new and extremely expensive satellite, but the sound lines would be carried by Cable & Wireless from Tokyo to the USA then to London. The BBC had sent a top team of 38 commentators and producers to Tokyo to add 'live' commentary to the day's edited highlights when they were transmitted to London. Day One OK. On Day Two a dredger – some say in Tokyo Bay, others say it was in Honolulu waters – cut through this expensive, valuable, essential cable. This happened about eleven in the morning, our time; the repair could take hours, but it may take days. The only way out was to add commentary live in our London studio. But most of our 'experts' were in Tokyo.

The next few hours were frantic, to say the least.

Norris McWhirter came up from his holiday home in Cornwall.

Dorian Williams, taking a break because of over-work, came in from his equestrian home.

Cliff Morgan.   © EMPICS

Harry Walker came out of retirement to give the Olympics one last go.

Simon Smith, from Birmingham, caught the next train down to London.

To add authenticity to our efforts we roped in Len Martin, the 'voice' to read any official results behind the Tokyo pictures. Besides covering their own sport, they also commentated on cycling, judo, wrestling and weight-lifting.

'Cliffy' worked harder for those six transmissions than he had ever worked on the rugby field. He was in his element. Race reading for Norris, timing the turns in the pool for Harry, urging Simon on for the last thirty seconds of a round and adding his knowledge of showjumping for Dorian. They were all magnificent. Simply wonderful. Now that was where years of cool calm broadcasting experience was used.

But what of our 'talent' back in Tokyo? The Colemans, the Pickerings, David Vine, Alan Weeks, Peter West, Max Robertson, to name a few. Each day they would sit in an 'Off-tube' commentary position within the Tokyo Olympics Broadcasting Centre, commentating to pictures of the day's happenings.

Their words got no further than Tokyo Bay.

Mexico, October 1968. About 25 of us arrived a week or so before the Games started. It was a long flight in those days, 13 hours. One of our crowd, producer Ricky Tilling, wanted to look around the city, so he dumped his bags in his room and went on the town, listening to the ever-chanting mariachis, and in particular, trying out Mexican dishes from the roadside vendors.

He returned to the hotel in the wee early hours. Ever heard of Montezuma's revenge? Ricky had within a few hours of returning to his room, where he remained until the day we returned to London,

BBC TV team of the 1968 Mexico Olympic Games.
(The good looking, intelligent members in the rear.)

168

two and a half weeks later! I saw him, once. I went up to his room after ten days and eventually he came to the door. He was grey; his cheeks, his eyes, his lips, all grey. He just mumbled, 'I'm dying,' and shut the door.

Two members of the team who kept clear of Montezuma's revenge were fellow producer Alan Mouncer and me. We were producing the athletics together, which was taking place at the magnificent Aztec Stadium; coverage of all the events was provided by Mexican television. We were in a large commentary box together with David Coleman, Ron Pickering, Stuart Storey and Mary Rand, GB's '64 gold medallist. Alan and I, between us, were deciding who did which commentary on which event as it came onto the screen. There were dozens of events happening at the same time. Our selection was transmitted, via satellite, to London.

Just two boxes away were the ITV commentary team. We were having a lot of hard competition from ITV; in 1968 it was at its strongest. The previous night at the Athletics Olympic Village, we found the tyres of our vehicles had been slashed when we tried to leave with gold medallist David Hemery on board. We had no transport, so ITV stepped in and whisked Hemery away. Important though David Hemery was, the story of the Games was the rise of Black Power. American athletes Smith and Carlos had won the gold and silver medals in the 400 metres and, as they stood on the medal rostrum, had raised a clenched fist with head bowed as the salute of the so-called oppressed black athletes. It caused sensational ripples within the Olympic Games, indeed throughout the world of sport. ITV had already beaten us to the punch by grabbing a filmed interview with these two famous athletes down in the Olympic village. Smith and Carlos, incidentally, were then expelled by their country from the American team camp and from any further participation with the American team. But not only were they available for interviews with the media, so too were their wives, who had now joined their husbands.

Smith and Carlos came to work with us in the BBC commentary box, and, though at times it seemed that the whole of the world's press were also trying to talk to them, the two famous athletes were exclusive to us, the BBC. We were using them as summarisers, adding their comments and thoughts on the various happenings down on the track.

Track and field ran from about 11 a.m. until 6 p.m. every day.

Both Alan and I realised that at the end of each day the whole of the media, written and electronic, would descend upon our commentary box. So we devised a plan to leave a good 45 minutes before the finish. Coleman and Co. had worked on enough Olympics to manage for 45 minutes on their own. Our car was brought up to the rear of the stadium, just behind the commentary boxes. Suddenly we ran, darting in and out of the various levels of the stadium, swerving past startled spectators, followed by perhaps half a dozen media men, but gradually leaving them behind. We were led by two of the fastest men in the world, who every so often glanced back at us just for reassurance of the direction they should take. We made the car in record time and then left in completely the opposite direction; the five of us, with our driver, in this roomy, powerful limousine.

Our driver was superb, speeding like hell through the Mexico City suburbs towards the outer ring road. We had just reached it when up zoomed a huge motorcycle cop. He slowed in front of us, stopped and got off his machine. He was big, very big. Even though it was getting late in the evening he wore dark glasses. I was sure I had seen him before in a James Cagney or Humphrey Bogart film. He came back to our limo and leant right into the front passenger window, which our driver had slid open. He jerked his head, a signal for our driver to gabble away in Mexican Spanish for 30 seconds at least, before suddenly stopping and turning to us: 'Give me fifty dollars.' We did. He quickly put it into a newspaper and passed it to the motorcycle cop, who put the contents in his top breast pocket and threw the newspaper on the ground. Legally speaking, money had not been passed from hand to hand. 'The Aristos Hotel, you say,' said our motorcycle cop in a broad American accent. 'Si, Señor,' said our driver.

Then we started a drive which had even Smith and Carlos gasping for breath. Obviously our driver had spilled all the beans. And it worked. Led by our policeman, with his siren roaring loudly, we travelled sometimes, I thought, at the speed of light. We seemed to reach our hotel, the Aristos, which was practically in the centre of Mexico City, within 20 minutes. By the time we had got Smith and Carlos out of our car and gone through the front of the hotel, our motorcycle cop was standing there offering a salute. 'That in itself is worth another fifty dollars,' said Alan. (It didn't take us long to understand the Mexican way of working, the way of getting things done.)

A double suite had been put aside in advance for Smith and Carlos and their respective wives. Once they were all safely ensconced, Alan and I departed for the bar. It was deserted, apart from one other, familiar face, that of Ron Pickering. 'You two look knackered,' said Ron, and he quickly ordered us a drink. Alan agreed. I just grunted and took a long pull at my drink. 'I've got just the answer for you both. Come on, finish up and follow me.'

To cut a long story short we ended up down in the basement. Stripped. In a sauna. Then into an ice-cold shower. Then, ten minutes later, all three of us were lying on our respective massage tables, side by side, completely naked, being pummelled to death by three hefty masseurs. The pummelling, and above all the kneading of the muscles, was absolutely bliss. The phone rang and one of the masseurs brought it to me. It was Alan Chivers, our executive producer, speaking from the broadcasting centre. 'Alec, I've just been tipped off that an ITV camera and interviewing team are in our hotel, the Aristos, and are up on the top floor trying to get to Smith and Carlos to interview them. Stop them. I don't mind what methods you use. Just stop them!' The line went dead.

I quickly relayed the news to Ron and Alan. We all dressed in record time. As we were going up in the lift to the 12th floor, I looked hard at Alan and Ron, both just staring at the lift door. Alan was lean, hard and fit. Ron Pickering was six foot two, with a bullet chest of about 52 inches and muscles like iron. It was no secret that I could handle myself. I estimated that there would be about five or six ITV fellows. 'It will be murder,' I thought.

The lift doors opened. We tore out, looking left and right. There was Jonathan Martin, then a lowly PA, later to become Head of Sport, dancing up and down, clutching his testicles in one hand and shouting, 'They are in there, suite twelve-forty.' And so doing he quickly disappeared into his own room opposite and slammed the door.

We hit the door of suite 1240 all together, a combined weight of just over 40 stone. The door just splintered open. Seven pairs of eyes looked at us, startled. The first to speak was David Coleman. He was pouring tea. 'Come in, lads, you're just in time to join us for tea.'

Smith and Carlos were in another room. Coleman, anticipating a bloodbath, quite rightly, had taken the ITV crew aside and was calmly, quietly and rationally sorting out the problem. He looked like a pussy cat. He prevented the day from ending with headline ferocity.

Boxer Chris Finnegan won the middleweight title at the Mexico City Games. Half an hour later, in his dressing room, after all the hullabaloo had died down and Chris himself was coming down to earth a little, I asked him, 'Chris, we have a satellite up in 2½ hours. That is half past ten. OK to interview you straight to London?' 'Sure, save me the cost of ringing the missus and telling her. I'll do it on the air,' cackled an excited Chris. He still had this cheerful, but terribly dedicated, medical official with him from the IOC staff, in charge of doping. This didn't worry laid-back Chris Finnegan, Olympic Champion.

Now, as everyone can recall, in 1968 the winners of Olympic titles had to take a doping test, i.e. they provided a specimen of urine immediately after the event and before participating in any other activity. Which included eating and sex. Though Chris had tried to provide he hadn't been successful so far. Relax, said everyone around him, and he was given a huge bottle of Perrier water to get stuck into. This he did. He showered and dressed. He finished that bottle and started on another one, then attended the press conference accompanied by his bottle. His fight had finished about 7.30 p.m. It was now approaching nine o'clock. Still nothing. We had a long talk to the IOC officials (there were two of them by then), pointing out the importance, and cost, of our specially booked satellite. It was 9.30 p.m. We had to get going to the studio. Bottle of water number three was now being clutched by Chris. We tore through the Mexico City traffic; Mexican taxi drivers can only drive at 60 mph. We got there at 10.15. 'Try walking up and down, Chris.' Chris did that in between huge gulps of water. The bottles were enormous, at least a litre. The two IOC officials were jabbering away at each other, talking ninety to the dozen. Officially they had to stay within two metres of the gold medallist. There was nothing for it but to let them each sit either side of Chris during the interview. Everything was explained to Harry Carpenter. For the next 10 minutes, until we went on the air, we tried every method we could think of to get Britain's new Olympic Champion to pee.

The interview had just started, when all of a sudden Chris, who normally had a lot to say for himself, started drying up, started to get almost embarrassed, squirming, his feet sliding from one side

172

of the chair he was sitting on to the other. I realised what was about to happen, 'Quickly,' I shouted to our videotape operator, 'go into a replay of the whole fight.' So, right in the middle of the interview, very nearly in the middle of a Harry Carpenter question, we suddenly cut to a replay of the fight.

Chris shot out of his chair shouting, 'Where, where?' Someone pointed down the corridor. He dashed down, closely followed by the two IOC officials, both with their bottles. They were gone a long time, nearly 10 minutes. A happy-looking Chris Finnegan finally reappeared, relaxed and looking as if a weight was off his mind. Our two IOC officials took their leave. Chris was now the official Middleweight Champion, having peed into a bottle during a live interview from Mexico to London.

For me, the Montreal Olympics in 1976 were different for three reasons. One, though you were English the locals never spoke to you unless you addressed them in French. Two, the security. Following the horrific killings of members of the Israeli team at the previous Olympics, in Munich in '72, security was understandable, but nevertheless extremely tough. Not only was one's accreditation checked when entering or leaving an Olympic venue, but the many hundreds of armed soldiers amplified the importance of the occasion. At some events there were more security men than competitors. The third reason involved, to a certain extent, a little something of both of the above, language and security.

Each morning the EBU produced a two-hour tape of the previous day's events; this included what we, the BBC, and the viewer, regarded as rather minor sports. Shooting was one of these, though one never knew when a GB participant might pull a rabbit out of the bag. The first 20 minutes of these highlights consisted of the previous day's shooting events. Peter West, who knew nothing about shooting, was assigned the task of commentating on this segment every morning, and I had to look after him. So I approached Dick Palmer, Deputy Secretary of the British team, who I had known for many, many years. Dick suggested the British competitor in the first shooting event, the free pistol, one Laslo Antal. A quick word the day before the games started brought forth, 'Delighted, old boy, I'm only in this one event and will get knocked out early, and I am then free for the next ten days.'

So Dr Laslo Antal, a short, muscular, fortyish dentist from Liverpool, became our shooting expert sitting alongside Peter every morning, advising off mic, translating complicated events into simple layman's terms. He did this very well, much to Peter's satisfaction and relief, and every morning about 5.45, our little British competitor would be waiting for us at the studio door. A quick look at the running order and we would be on air via satellite to England, with Peter West relating events with all the eloquence that only he could give them, and little Laslo sitting alongside him chattering away ninety to the dozen. Incidentally, he came 12th in his event, the free pistol, the best placing of all the British team in the shooting events. And his broadcasting task was just as successful. Until one day...

About five days in we arrived a little later than usual. The long hours were beginning to take their toll on us, but Laslo was hopping around in a very excited manner. As soon as there was the slightest pause in the conversation he would dive in with, 'I must tell you something. Last night...' Not now, Laslo,' I warned. Let's get this shooting on the air. It's complicated enough without all this chatter.' He was not subdued, and like a little rubber ball he bounced in with a further attempt. One expected to hear about some female athletes spending all night in the male quarters, or vice versa. We went on the air. Laslo shut up and concentrated on the job in hand. Once the item was over, however, he opened his mouth, but I jumped in with a 'Let's all go up to the canteen and sit down with some coffee and toast. Then, Laslo, you can tell us your news.'

This was Laslo Antal's story.

'So I was lying in bed chatting away to my room-mate. Apart from this BBC stint we had both been at a loose end since our events had finished. It was just coming up to eleven-thirty. We heard the camp helicopter come in to land and shut down for the night. The previous evening we had wandered over to the helicopter pad and been there when one of these heavily armed choppers had come in, had watched whilst the crew of three had switched off and clambered out: the pilot, the navigator and gunner, all dressed in black, light overalls and wearing earmuffs. Flying around in one of these noisy choppers for hour after hour would severely affect one's hearing unless one's eardrums were protected. And they were, with large, tight muffs. So there we were, lying in the dark, chatting about some competition or other, when all of a sudden there was a bang. Another bang. A shot. Two shots in all. We both recognised the sound of a shot being fired from a 7.62mm automatic rifle.

'We quickly threw on some clothes and dashed out in the direction of the helicopter pad. As fast as we were, others were faster. By the time we began to get close to the pad there were swarms of military about, and, though we ducked and dived around first one opening and then another, our way was always barred by at least two security guards. White-coated hospital or ambulance orderlies and doctors began to appear. So we changed tactics. We split up and just wandered around within that area. Eavesdropping. Nothing more. Occasionally asking a passing soldier or airman, even a medical orderly.

' "Two fellows left as soon as it touched down ... the pilot and navigator ... the gunner stayed behind..." *As they passed, one picked up the conversation.* "He was about 28, a sergeant gunner ... he was at least five minutes later..." *It was a word here, a sentence there.* "He was unloading his gun ... he was packing up his ammunition ... he was very loaded up when he left the chopper..." *Bit by bit we were putting the pieces together.* "He was still wearing the muffs ... they say he was challenged when he was a dozen steps from the chopper..." *Sometimes the comments were whispered or muffled, at other times quite loud.* "If it was in French or English, who knows ... they say he didn't speak French ... he was challenged again ... in English, I'm sure..." *It was taking time but it was coming together.* "He still carried on... Some say he was challenged a third time ... in French... Someone else said the guard was a rookie, new to the Army ... only about 19... Nobody wanted to do guard duty that night ... they said they aimed at his legs ... he was hit once in the stomach ... once in the chest ... he was dead when he hit the ground ... still wearing his earmuffs..."

'It was 4 a.m. by the time we had pieced all the little bits together. We dashed over to our HQ block. Got one of our senior staff out of bed. Told him. He didn't want to know. "More trouble on our shoulders?" So here I am telling you the story, and I think it is one hell of a story.'

So did I. I dashed up to the BBC's complex of offices on the fourth floor. Sam Leitch had just arrived. I grabbed him and briefed him on the way down to the canteen. I asked Laslo to repeat his story. Sam sat and listened, now and again just punctuating the telling by a quick question. He looked from one to the other. 'If I was still working for the *Mirror* I would definitely use this story, but I'm not. I haven't got enough evidence to say for sure that someone was shot last night. I have still got a few guys on the Montreal press who owe me a favour, though. I'll get them to ask around.' But we never used it.

Towards the end of the year, about December, Sam guided me into his office and sat me down with my favourite drink, a large G & T. He threw me a telex, which had just arrived from a journalist contact on the *Montreal Times*, the leading newspaper of that city. It read: 'Hello, Sam. Hope this finds you well. Sorry this has taken so long, but here is the tale.' Entitled 'SECURITY SOLDIER ACCIDENTALLY KILLED DEFENDING OLYMPIC ATHLETES', the article, which finally substantiated Laslo's story, read in part as follows:

So, two of the three soldiers, the pilot and navigator, climbed out of the chopper, while the gunner, a sergeant, stayed behind to completely dismantle his gun and remove the shells. He was walking from the plane whistling away, quite loudly. He still had his earmuffs on. It was dark but he knew his way back across the strip to the air control. He was challenged by a security guard, a fairly young guard: 'Halt. Identify yourself.' No reply, just faint whistling. 'Halt. Identify yourself.' Once again nothing. The helicopter gunner stood out in the backlit half-light from the Olympic village. Once again he was challenged. No reply. Bang. Bang. Two shots were fired. One pierced his stomach, the other his heart. He was dead before he hit the ground, still wearing his earmuffs.

When a little dentist from Liverpool tells you something – listen.

Lake Placid, a little town 250 miles north of New York, nestling amidst the Adirondack Mountains, the American town where John Brown's body lies. This was the destination, the host town, of the 1980 Winter Olympics.

We arrived 14 days before the Games began, we being contracts manager, Mike Dolbear, my assistant, Lesley Morris, and I. I assigned all three of us to our luxurious condominiums. Lovely place, Lake Placid, and charming people, but the accommodation for the Olympics was abysmal – no, appalling. Competitors were housed in the Lake Placid house of correction. Brand new, sure, but nevertheless it was intended to be the jail when the last of the Olympic competitors had left. The press, written and electronic, were allocated two-star boarding houses, two to a room, at $90 per night. Eighteen months earlier I had rented 10 condominiums for a $3\frac{1}{2}$-week duration at $1,000 each! I signed the contract with shaking hands. As it was, considering the usual Olympic inflation, I finished up with the bargain of the Games, because our accommodation worked out at $50 a night per person for our team of 23.

So I insisted, in my luxury condominium, that on our first full day we would recce the Olympic sites. The temperature was about 10 degrees below freezing, but if we kept going we would be OK. We went here, there and everywhere, and by 3.30 p.m. there was only the bob run to see. I cracked the whip and off we sped. By 4 o'clock it was getting distinctly chilly, by 4.30, when we were just finishing, it was freezing. We were all like icebergs. The bob run was just on the edge of town, so a pub or a wine bar was not far away. We found one, lovely and warm inside, but we were still very frozen. I quickly explained our predicament, adding 'We are from England'. The bartender looked, started to give us a lecture, then reached above his head for a square bottle of yellowish liquid, poured out three small shots and said, 'Drink that down in one'. We did. None of us felt it go down our throats and gullets into our stomachs. 'Want another one?' We nodded. 'Sip this one.' Just then all three of us felt this warm, warm glow spreading outwards, upwards and downwards from the centre of our stomachs. We relaxed, and began to undo our outer garments. I picked up the bottle from the bar: 'Yukon Jack 100°-proof Canadian Liquor, made with Canadian Whisky – "The Black Sheep of Canadian Liquors"'. We all started chatting away, either to ourselves or to the barman. Another round came. To cut a long, unruly story short, after three of these each we were all paralytic, legless. Never in my life have I been in this state after just three drinks, and very small glasses too. Thank God the British press had yet to arrive in Placid. How we got back to our condominiums, who drove back, etc., I do not know. We all quietly met up the following morning.

If you ever get cold, really cold, take a slug of Yukon Jack and I guarantee you will be a different person. On the back of the

177

bottle it reads, 'Yukon Jack is a taste born of hoary nights, when lonely men struggled to keep their fires lit and cabins warm'.

The Games were being covered by ABC of America, and from two weeks before the start hundreds of technicians were installing their cables and cameras and microphones, even on the downhill ski run. The cable from the previous year's runs had been left installed on the latter, and it had been hoped that all that would be required was for the cameras or mics to be plugged in along the route; but the chipmunks had other ideas. The red, yellow and green cables attracted these funny little animals, and they must have tasted all right too, because the word went out and during America's Thanksgiving and Christmas holidays these little friends from the animal world ate 28 miles of cable! Only thousands of bits were left, so the whole of the men's downhill, the first Olympic event, had to have the cables relaid.

One morning, when the temperature was really low, I watched for a few minutes. The cameramen hauled their cameras up to the top of the ski jump, two cameras positioned right at the top, 250 feet high. One big strapping cameraman was hauling away, and his efforts were bringing forth clouds and clouds of steamy breath from his mouth and nostrils. He was way up at the top of the jump when suddenly he stopped. He collapsed. He had been working all alone at the top. It took three to four to minutes for a couple of his colleagues to reach him. They had already called for an ambulance, which came racing in, three paramedics also having to haul themselves up to the top. He was stretchered and carefully but quickly slid down the slope to waiting hands below, into the ambulance, which with sirens screeching tore off to Lake Placid's hospital. The paramedics at the top had confirmed that he was dead, his heart had stopped; it was also confirmed at the hospital. Nevertheless, he was rushed into resuscitation. He had just been placed on the table when his whole body started shaking. Half a dozen pairs of hands started to tear his clothes off. As they did, perspiration started pouring down his face and body. His eyelids started to flicker, then snapped open. For 12 whole minutes this big, strong, strapping lad to all intents and purposes – certainly to the medics that took his pulse for those 12 minutes – was DEAD. His lungs had frozen with the effort he had been putting into hauling up the equipment. His lungs being wide open, and the temperature being 20 degrees or so below, just froze. He was kept inside for a few days, but before the Games had finished he was covering the top of the ski jumps, as planned, for ABC television.

Editor Bob Abrahams, from the time he arrived in Lake Placid, had been pestering me to obtain aerial shots of Lake Placid and the competition sites. Security was tight and the only commercial helicopter over the venues belonged to ABC, who were reluctant to loan it to us for a couple of hours. Time was getting short. Then I suddenly had one of my many brilliant brainwaves. I put a call through to Wolverhampton and to Goodyear UK. I spoke to my contact, with whom I had a very good understanding resulting from our use of the Goodyear Airship during the previous five years. He assured me that the Goodyear Airship HQ would contact me within a very short time. Within the hour I was speaking to a Tim Owen, from Florida. 'Hello, Mr Owen, it is nice of you to ring me. As I was explaining to Reg at Wolverhampton, I am in desperate need of aerial shots of Lake Placid. We have a preview programme and we are desperate to show off this beautiful town of Lake Placid.' I thought a little bullshit about America wouldn't do any harm.

'Call me Tim, Mr Weeks. Now, tell me, is this all in connection with the Winter Olympics?'

'Why, yes. The skating, the bob, the skiing, the ski jumping and so on and so on. We want to show as much as we can of these events from the air.'

'Reg was explaining to me, Mr Weeks, that you are one of our main users of the airship in the UK.' Now, who was bullshitting whom? After a grunt from me he went on.

'This is terribly exciting, Mr Weeks. The picture you are painting would be quite fantastic and have a wonderful effect on the screen.' My heart jumped. I've got him, I thought. Hook, line and sinker. I really am very persuasive.

'Tell me, Mr Weeks, is it cold in Lake Placid?'

'I should say so, real brass-monkey weather,' and him being American I added, 'about 15 degrees below.'

'Have you got snow up there, Mr Weeks?'

'Of course we've got snow up here,' I said, thinking the man was an idiot. 'These are the Winter Olympics. You need snow.'

'Well, Mr Weeks, this would be a wonderful project to work on. You paint a very exciting picture. Unfortunately, there is only one little problem, Mr Weeks. You say it is very cold up there, Mr Weeks, the airship is filled with helium, and when the helium gets cold, Mr Weeks, it freezes, and when it freezes, Mr Weeks, it slides to the nose of the ship, Mr Weeks, and when that happens, Mr Weeks, it would be difficult to fly as it would be nosediving all the time. But, Mr Weeks, if you get the Winter Olympics switched to Florida you could certainly, Mr Weeks, use the Goodyear Airship! I'll wait to hear from you.' Then he rang off.

I felt four inches tall. I gave the pilot of the ABC helicopter $500 and he got our shots for us. He never even called me Mr Weeks once.

On the day of the opening ceremony, besides various 'feeds', one monitor of the sixteen in front of me in our control room carried the output of a portable camera just outside the main stadium door. This camera was for special shots of the Olympic Flame and of the specially selected athlete, representing the youth and fitness of the Americans, who would carry the Flame on its last full lap around the stadium, then up the steps to light the Olympic torch of these Winter Games.

One thing that has never ceased to set my adrenalin flowing is the journey of the Olympic Flame. From Mount Olympus in Greece, handed by relay runner to relay runner. Sure, it had to be flown by plane over the seas, but once on its new continent the steady stream of runners took over, and this was how it was for the 1980 Winter Olympics in Lake Placid, USA.

The opening ceremony had been going for some 30 minutes or so. Soon the Olympic Flame would appear through the main arena gates. Then our attention was drawn to the picture on the monitor of the portable camera just outside the main gates. A few people, four all told, were in shot; one, a strapping, tall, well-built athletic-looking fellow in his mid-twenties, mouthed a request for a cigarette. An official produced a large windproof type of cigarette lighter and our athlete lit up. He was dressed in a white polo-necked sweater with red sleeves and bright blue ski trousers, the tight-fitting type. Red, white and blue, America's national colours. All four kept looking at their watches. Now, remember, this picture was not being transmitted. Only we were privileged to see the camera's output. Another look at watches, another drag on the cigarette by our young man. The fanfares boomed out from within the stadium, its sounds reverberating over beautiful Lake Placid and indeed, because of modern telecommunications, via satellite throughout the world. Our athlete took a last drag, stamped out his fag, removed his tracksuit, and bent down and picked up an object that had been lying at his feet. It was an unlit Olympic torch. The official stepped forward, produced his large silver windproof cigarette lighter and 'Whoosh!', the torch leapt into flame. Our young man trotted toward the stadium gates, which, on cue, swept open as 25,000 people stood and thundered out their approval at the sight of this athlete carrying the torch (lit by a cigarette lighter five seconds earlier and not, as one imagined, carried by a fleet of relay runners from Mount Olympus), moving towards the top of the stadium to light the Olympic Flame, which was to burn for 11 days.

Do you believe in Santa Claus?

In every team there is always one. Lake Placid was no exception. A nicer man you could not know. A greater colleague you never had. A fine commentator, an equally good reporter and one of the world's foremost experts on tennis. How BBC Radio came to select their one and only representative for the 1980 Winter Olympics I do not know. His name was Gerald Williams.

Now, that would normally be OK, but on our team we had a Ron Pickering and a David Vine, and two of the world's most wicked leg-pullers you could not wish to know. Whenever they saw Gerald their faces lit up. Their thoughts were obvious, focusing on two 'events'.

The downhill: there is no greater, no more death-defying, no more thrilling event in the whole of the Olympic Games than the downhill skiing event. The individual competitors in either the women's or men's events took their very lives into their hands.

The luge and toboggan are also exciting, not only the speeds which are reached around the run, but also the competitors' outfits. The competitors' clothing is made from a piece of synthesised rubber so thin it is practically transparent – the thickness reminds me of something whose name escapes me. Nothing is worn underneath. Therefore, in either the men's or women's events nothing is left to one's imagination, and I mean nothing.

Right! Got the scene? Vine and Pickering had.

So we were halfway through the Games when they struck. 'Gerry, old boy,' says Vine on the talkback from the alpine skiing event to Gerald Williams sitting in the radio office back in our control room. 'Gerry, I wonder if you could do me a favour.' 'Of course, old man,' says Gerry, only too pleased to be assisting someone from the big TV team. 'What is it?'

'Could you pop along to that big office in the IBC (international broadcasting centre) and get the starting list for the mixed pairs downhill, the event where they go downhill holding hands.'

'I'll go along now and try to get you the starters before you leave the commentary position.' And off he goes. Now, just the thought of a male and female skier hurtling down the slope at 50 mph, holding hands, has us all in fits of laughter. Gerry in the meantime, and for the next two hours, is pulling the information bureau to bits searching for the starters' list of the mixed pairs downhill.

He apologises to David Vine when he sees him that evening, explaining the lengths he went to. 'Don't worry old boy,' says Vine. 'I've got a starting list now. Thanks for trying.'

So a few days later it is Ron Pickering's turn. Gerry, as usual ensconced within the radio office at the IBC, receives a call. 'Gerry, Ron here. I'm speaking from the speed-skating.'

'Yes, Ron, how can I help you?' says the ever-enthusiastic Gerry.

'This event is going to go on all day. Could you possibly do me a favour and get me a starting list which I need for tomorrow.'

'Sure, Ron, what is it?'

'It's the starting list for the Olympic Final of the mixed luge. The men and women's event.' There is a silence. 'Did you get that, Gerry?'

'Of course, Ron. Sorry. I was scribbling everything down. I've got it, starting list for the final of the mixed luge. I'll get on to that immediately.'

Now, I'm hearing all this in my adjoining office. Just the thought of a woman lying on top of a man wearing those flimsy uniforms and travelling at 40 mph would make the event the most sexual activity of the Games. Of any Games. But Gerry's thoughts were innocently pure. He disappeared. It was about 11 o'clock in the morning. Pickering and Gerry Williams took a back seat in my mind for the rest of that day, until about 6.30 that evening, when I spoke to a very flustered Frenchman, the Head of the Eurovision Information Bureau.

'Weeks, we have a problem. Your Mr Gerald Williams, he has been in the bureau since this morning asking for,' the Frenchman consulted his notes, 'the starting list of the Olympic Final of the mixed luge.' He stopped speaking as he looked at me. 'You know,' Mr Weeks, there is no such event. No such thing. We all laughed when he first mentioned it, but after some while we realised he was very serious.' He broke off to mumble something in French. 'I tried to explain to him that this event would be impossible, and why, and that even in France we would not allow such an event. Your Mr Williams is a very gifted person. When he arrived he spoke to us in English. After some time in French. Then in German. When he was getting nowhere he turned to Italian, then Spanish. When I left the bureau just now he was trying to make himself understood in halting Russian.' Our friend sat down exhausted.

I later went and rescued Gerry from the information office, brought him back to his own office and made sure he spoke to Ron Pickering, who by now was back from the speed-skating and warmly ensconced in his comfortable condominium. I listened on the extension phone.

Ron, I am sure, very nearly had an uncontrollable fit. Years later tears would still spring to his eyes when we recalled the starting list for the mixed luge.

Gerry is still pure, and innocent. And 'one'...

And you did not have to be a commentator to be 'one' ... you could be a competitor.

So Ron Pickering was just approaching his fifth and final day of speed-skating, held at the outdoor speed-skating oval in brilliant sunshine on all five days. Though it snowed heavily at night, it only took a short time to sweep the snow from the rink into huge piles, especially on the corners, where they reached eight to ten feet high. Though it was bitterly cold, the sun was so bright the competitors often raced against their own reflections. The setting was perfect, especially for the sensation of the Games, Eric Heiden of the USA. Four gold medals, one in every speed-skating event, and he was coming up to the final and fastest event of them all, the blue riband of the ice rink – the 500 metres. Ron was doing his commentary live on the satellite link, live to London videotape machines for transmission a few hours later. The link was costing something like £45 per minute.

The four skaters were on the ice: Heiden on the inside lane, a

Russian, a Dutchman and one from Great Britain. Archie Marshall had been 40th and last in his other event, the 1,000 metres, but this would be his great test, competing against the magnificent Eric Heiden. The British boy had drawn the short straw by having the outside lane. As they started in an echelon formation, it would be the only time that the outside lane would be in front of the inside. Ron started his commentary. 'And so the great Eric Heiden crouches down for this, his final race, in an attempt to win his fifth gold medal. Archie Marshall in the outside lane represents Great Britain in this final race of the speed-skating events. They're poised.' *BANG.* 'They're off. Heiden bursts out of the start as if jet-propelled and is hurling himself forward towards the first bend. So indeed is the British boy, Archie Marshall...'

Ron stopped commentating. I could see why. I could see the pictures on the monitor. His voice was now becoming a stifled convulsion. Whilst Heiden is tearing around the rink the British boy is attempting to match the American's speed on the turn. He didn't. He couldn't turn. When he hit the bend at a speed he had never achieved before in his life he just kept going, and going. And going. He shot off the ice and dived right into the pile of freshly swept snow lying six foot high by the side of the rink. All that could be seen of the British skater was a pair of flailing legs and skates. Ron Pickering started laughing. Not a quiet laugh, not subdued, but a full belly laugh as only Ron Pickering could give.

The two engineers alongside me in the control room started laughing. The producer – alongside Ron – started laughing. I picked up the phone to talk to London and all I could hear, 5,000 miles away, were people laughing. It just went on and on. And all the time the camera remained riveted by this pair of legs that were still flapping frantically in this heap of snow. Ron's laughter had now reached hysterical levels. He sounded as if he was about to have a fit.

The legs carried on waving. Yes, our skater was definitely 'one'. I started laughing.

Robin Cousins, skating fourth in the final five-minute event of the Men's Olympic Championship, sat on a cushion in the corridor leading onto the rink, reading a detective novel. When called onto the ice he calmly folded the page, put down his book and went out and skated to a Gold Medal.

The following morning, about 10 o'clock, I arrived at the broadcasting centre with my assistant, Lesley Morris. The BBC complex of offices was at the far corner, on the first floor of the bus garage that had been turned into the international broadcasting centre. It normally took us two minutes to walk from the main door of the building to our offices. The day following Robin's gold-medal-winning performance it took us 15 fifteen minutes; the Russians were hugging us; the Danes were slapping us on the back; the Germans were shaking our hands; the Italians were kissing us. Everyone was congratulating us as if we had won the medal. Within this building, the IBC, there are no barriers, no political walls; whether you understand one another or not, everyone is equal. I've experienced this ever since I've worked on the major events, starting with the Wembley Olympics in 1948. If hardened professional broadcasters can make it work, why not the world's politicians?

Moscow. My first visit there was in April 1978; all told I made 11 visits between then and the start of the Games in July 1980.

Right from the start I found Alexander Ivanitsky, their Head of Sport, and his whole department, very professional in their approach to the organisation of the broadcasting of the Games. Any visiting broadcaster with production experience would be asked to chat to a few of their directors and senior cameramen. This few would be 70 or 80 per lecture, which would last for 90 minutes, followed by a further hour of question time.

My lecture was on soccer, and right at the end I asked a question of one particularly persistent director. 'I've talked on and off about soccer for nearly two hours. What have you gained from this?' Answer, through the interpreter: 'If we can learn one new shot, one new camera angle every day, we will be very well informed by the time the Games begin.'

One had to be very patient at meetings with Gostelradio, as the Russians called their Olympic TV and radio consortium. For example, three to four weeks prior to one of my visits a telex was sent from us, itemising all the questions and points we needed to raise. These sometimes amounted to as many as a hundred various matters we wanted to discuss during our six-day visit – always six days, never longer. Approximately 60 per cent of our questions would be answered, the remainder to be left until our next visit two months' later.

From April 1978 steady progress was made during the following 18 months, including the solution to a very delicate request for extra facilities. It was essential for our commentators at the athletics and gymnastics to see the output of our studio on the monitors. We had to have our own reverse vision from our Moscow studio to the Lenin Stadium, five miles away. So we did a deal with the Russians. We would give them a piece of equipment which they desperately required.

It was valued at about £48,000 and produced digital effects; that is, different pictures on the screen at the same time, the same picture breaking into 16 separate pictures, or 4 or 8, etc. In return the Russians would give us a special circuit carrying our studio output back to our commentators at the Lenin Stadium.

Then came 26th December 1979. The invasion of Afghanistan by the Russians, by the Soviet Army, to be precise. At first it was just another serious political row, but though politics and sport do not normally mix President Carter was determined they would. He, the President, was due to declare open the 1980 Winter Olympics at Lake Placid. In mid-January he deputised Vice-President Mondale for this; then two days after the Games finished the United States officially boycotted the forthcoming Moscow Olympics, calling for all 'free-speaking democratic countries to do likewise'.

The Prime Minister, Mrs Margaret Thatcher, duly requested the British Olympic Association to follow in the footsteps of our American brethren and also announced other restrictions, which included breaking off all trade relations with the USSR and imposing a ban on all exports from Great Britain to the USSR. Sir Dennis Fellows, Chairman of the British Olympic Association, was as stubborn and as proud as a bulldog and had no intention of allowing politics to meddle with the hallowed Olympics. He announced that Great Britain would be sending a team. By 1st April the prospect of the BBC broadcasting the Moscow Games was in jeopardy.

The matter was to be settled finally by the Board of Governors after many, many hours of consultation with the government. In late April the IBA and BBC jointly announced that each would restrict its coverage to 52 hours of the total coverage. Even the size of broadcasting teams would be restricted to 60 each plus a

186

further 20 for radio. In all matters they complied with the wishes of the cabinet, including the exporting of equipment. This left our senior engineers and myself in a quandary. Whilst all the high-political 'government versus broadcasters' discussions were going on, we had to plan ahead and prepare as if we were covering the Games.

We couldn't just phone Gostelradio in Moscow: I knew all calls to Russia were being monitored and recorded at the BBC's monitoring station at Daventry; but via Televisa Mexicana, through Cuban TV, and then to Alexander Ivanitsky, Gostelradio's Head of Sport, we passed a message saying we would still get the equipment to him asap. With Mrs Thatcher's personally imposed ban on exports of all equipment of any nature to Russia, there was no way I could inform anyone in the BBC what we were doing. So the equipment was purchased (the payment of £48,000 having been authorised by a BBC senior director) and delivered in a suitcase which I imported into the USSR on a planning visit at the end of May. I think customs at Moscow knew what we were up to, as they passed us through all formalities within minutes – it normally took 50 to 60 minutes to clear Moscow customs and immigration. It still does to this day. The Quantel was installed and used for the first time on the first day of the competition. Successfully.

The Russians did a magnificent job on the Olympic Games. Both the organising of the event and the actual televising of the opening ceremony were mind-boggling in their magnificence. The TV coverage was directed by a slightly built 44-year-old woman, yet the British viewer saw only $16^{1/2}$ minutes of this two-and-a-quarter-hour event, by arrangement with the British Government. Politics won *that* day.

At the Cosmos Hotel during the period of the Games and the three weeks running up to it, one could get a breakfast of orange juice, coffee, fried, scrambled or boiled egg, toast and cereals. This is not normal in any Moscow hotel. The Cosmos Hotel overlooked the Moscow Constitutional Park and right in the forecourt of the park were two very large flower-beds. In one were the Olympic rings, the flowers blooming in the Olympic colours; in the other bed was the complete replica of the Russian Olympic mascot, Misha the Bear, a magnificent floral display. Even Percy Thrower would have agreed ... or Charlie Dimmock, if you're too young to recall Percy Thrower!

The security, however, was a nightmare.

All the children of Moscow were sent out of the city for 5 weeks, 18 days before the Games started, to health and holiday camps. The security troops ran the city. In spite of paying £42 per night for a room, we were all subjected to the X-ray airport-security type of machine, plus searching of all luggage, briefcase and handbags. This was on any occasion one wanted to enter one's own hotel, even at 2 a.m., which was the time that many of us returned from the broadcasting centre. To waste 15 minutes on this at the end of an exhausting day tried the patience of many of us, none more so than me.

Getting in and out of the international broadcasting centre was even worse. One had to go through this prolonged personal check going in and out. Unfortunately it often entailed waiting in the rain outside the main door whilst security slowly and methodically checked each individual. One could, to a certain extent, understand this, it being a high-security area. But the German television senior producer, who had a spinal injury he'd obtained during the war, couldn't walk or sit upright without his huge expansive body belt consisting of masses of small round-shaped aluminium strips. These held him together. Every day he had to go into a curtained enclosure and remove this supporting belt so that it could be checked by security. It took our German colleague 50 minutes each time to enter and 50 minutes each time to leave the building.

Sure, one's room was secretly searched every so often. You would have been a fool not to expect this. For example, I laid my shirts out carefully in the dressing-table drawer, and under each alternate shirt lapel I placed a handkerchief. Nine times during this seven-week stay my handkerchief and shirt routine were disturbed. This was proof that my room had been searched.

Five hundred security-force members, dressed in civilian clothing, lined the gangways of the Lenin Stadium every day. Both Lesley and I were always followed by a member of the international-relations department whenever we left the building. For every transmission a member of this same department was present in our control room. This illustrates the stupidity of the security and military personnel, and shows how they spoilt the friendly, open-handed pride and joy with which the normal Muscovites greeted every visitor.

Throughout the Games, meetings took place at all times of the day and night. It was particularly difficult with our Russian friends.

On one occasion, Alexander Ivanitsky asked for a meeting at 7.30 a.m., to discuss some of our complicated requirements, to which I took my ever-faithful assistant, Lesley Morris. We two sat with half a dozen Russians. Water was poured into glasses where we were sitting. Lesley took a sip and started coughing. I looked, I took a sip of my glass. It wasn't water, it was vodka. Now, vodka in Russia is lethal compared with the Russian vodka you can buy from the UK supermarkets. Each of our Russians in turn would name a toast, and one was expected to swig the glassful down in one gulp. I did and slammed the glass back onto the table, then carried on the discussion. I turned back to look at my glass. It was full again. Lesley had swapped our glasses. She had my empty glass, I had her full one. So our meeting of two hours covered four toasts, but to me that involved eight slugs of vodka. When we left I was whistling, humming and singing Kenny Ball's 'Midnight in Moscow' better than Kenny Ball can play it!

I could never understand why the BBC supplied air tickets, hotel accommodation and tickets for all nine days of track and field events for the so-called cousin of one of the British Team, who then gave ITV as many interviews as us. And, in any case, when they win a medal the competitor has to give an interview to all the press, written and electronic.

On the Tuesday evening after the Games had finished all was normal, as it had been for the past six weeks. On the Wednesday morning I was up at about 7.15 and pulled back the curtains from my 11th-floor window overlooking the Constitutional Park, but there were no Olympic Rings or Misha flower-beds. These had been replaced with a new magnificent floral work of art. In one bed the design of the hammer and sickle and in the other the face of Lenin. All the hundreds of flagpoles now carried these two emblems, not the Olympic Flag or Misha. Downstairs the restaurant offered Russian tea, black bread and goat's cheese. No sign of orange juice, eggs, toast, butter or jam.

Back to our room, having been gone 40 to 50 minutes: the lovely terylene towels had been replaced by the usual hessian cloth, and a harsh cardboard type of toilet paper had been installed in the loo. The Moscow Games were a memory, a dream which obviously the people had to forget. The authorities had organised and broadcast it so magnificently. Why could not these people bask in the light of the world's praise, or most of the world, anyway? After all,

189

within a few days of the end of the Games the politicians in the UK and USA had stopped screaming about Afghanistan.

I have a multitude of cameo memories of these Moscow Games.

My assistant Lesley received an official rebuke, a complaint from the international-relations department, for calling a member of the KGB a member of the KGB. In the USSR one was not supposed to call a spade a spade. On another occasion, I was phoned late at night by a member of the KGB. 'Would you please tell your broadcaster Mr—— not to exchange English currency for an excessive number of Russian roubles. Otherwise we must insist he departs for London on the first available plane.' One could receive three times the official rate of roubles for hard currency on the black market. Our 'brilliant' personality did it in broad daylight on the street corner. It was the same fellow who bought up all the leather jackets in Argentina and tried to fiddle his expenses in Spain! The true professional would take a taxi ride, and the driver, without a word being spoken, would give roubles in exchange for payment in dollars at three times the official rate.

Our leader in Moscow, BBC's Head of Sport, Alan Hart, was so concerned with secrecy over our transmission times that he refused to give me or my senior engineer, Norman Taylor, any of our transmission timings. So, ten days before the Games began we placed a call from Moscow to 35 Marylebone High Street, where 44 members of the editorial staff of the *Radio Times* were able to tell us just before that magazine went on sale to the public our exact hush-hush transmission times!

We hired 28 non-English-speaking Russian drivers. A dozen of them, during the early stages of the Games, gave us a great runaround, disappearing for the rest of the day after a simple early job. 'We did not understand,' they would always say through an interpreter. So I arranged for all of them to be on parade at 7.30 one morning. At the last moment I had to attend some EBU meeting, so young Lesley took the parade. I arrived back in time to witness this slightly-built Welsh lass marching up and down the ranks of these drivers, who were now standing to attention, looking petrified at the language pouring from her lips, – bad language in English – a little Russian and, most of all, a ripe old telling-off she gave them in Welsh. We had no trouble with the drivers after this.

Had the televising of the Games been worth it? To us, the BBC, yes, every minute of the $67^{1/2}$ hours we transmitted, which was

190

slightly more than the 52 hours the BBC's Board of Governors had guaranteed the government not to exceed. The complete final cost for these ill-fated Games came to £1.9 million, which was slightly less than the £2.6 million I had anticipated spending before Afghanistan blew up. This worked out at just over £28,000 per hour, which in 1980, compared with the standard light-entertainment costing of £65,000 per hour, was cheap television.

Finally, one small postscript: in 1978, on my first visit to Moscow, I contacted the British Embassy, introduced myself and explained the BBC's intentions. When the Afghanistan balloon went up they, the British Embassy, just did not want to speak to us, let alone see us. When I arrived just prior to the Games and wanted to see the Ambassador and explain what agreement the BBC had come to with the government, I was politely informed that the Ambassador did not think anything could be gained from our meeting, and refused to see me. On the day before the 1980 Games commenced he, the Ambassador, left Moscow on vacation. On 1st November 1985, 63-year-old Sir Curtis Keeble GCMG, former British Ambassador to Russia, 1978–1982, was appointed a governor of the BBC!

And a postscript to the final small postscript: It was November 1980, four months after the Moscow Games had ended, a Friday evening, about 8 o'clock, and pelting with rain. The doorbell went. 'Who the hell wants to go out on a night like this?' I said to my bulldog as I moved to the front door. There, standing in the porch, a six-footer, rain dripping off the edge of the trilby pulled down over his eyes, his coat collar turned up. I quickly glanced towards the gates and all I could see was a large, black limousine, though nothing inside as all the windows were darkened glass. 'Mr Weeks?' I nodded. 'Mr Alec Weeks of the BBC?' I agreed and stepped back at least to allow the visitor into the hall to shelter from the rain. He held up one hand to decline, and with the other he pulled a large envelope, practically a package, from his black-leather trench coat. 'Compliments of the USSR.' My hand clutched the package, he turned on his heel and was walking down the drive whilst I was still offering, 'Coffee, perhaps something stronger?' I was well stocked with Russian vodka. He got into the front passenger seat and the car glided away, with hardly a murmur from its engine.

Everything had happened so quickly, even the bulldog had made no inquisitive sniffs. There was no time. I shut the door and moved

191

down to the kitchen to open the large envelope. I pulled out a sheaf of papers. Headed 'COSMOS HOTEL – BBC MOVEMENTS'. The following nine foolscap pages contained the dates of arrival of each of the 80 members of the BBC team – TV and radio; the rooms they occupied; and each day when they arrived in those rooms and when they left them, including the time between midnight and 6 a.m. I had enough evidence for at least a dozen spouses to sue for divorce.

The BBC stood high in the estimation of the Russian Government. They knew that the BBC had gone 30 per cent above its allotted number of hours of Olympic broadcasting, and this was their way of handing on information that in Russia would be invaluable. After thoroughly reading it, twice, I put it away somewhere safe.

Even before the ink was dry on the 1980 accounts, I was making arrangements to visit Los Angeles, where the 1984 Summer Olympics had been awarded, but in the February of that same Olympic year, 1984, the Winter Olympics were staged at Sarajevo.

So much has taken place in the Olympic city of Sarajevo since that opening ceremony, which had promised so much hope and prosperity to millions of Yugoslavs. Today there is hardly anything left standing that reminds one of those happy and colourful times. The Yugoslavs televised the Games very well indeed: the ice hockey, speed-skating, skiing, bob and luge runs – everything except for one thing, one event, one sport.

They positioned their cameras perfectly, and captured the magnificent excitement of the downhill, the frightening speed of the luge and bob runs, and the exhaustion of the cross-country events; but the coverage of the figure skating was pathetic, to say the least, and, as you may recall, the one event where we fancied our chances was in the figure skating, specifically the ice dancing – Torvill and Dean. Since the Lake Placid Olympics, where they were fifth, Torvill and Dean had won practically everything that was available to be won: the European and World titles, in fact everything except the Olympics, and I was determined that the world of television, especially the millions at home in the UK, would see Torvill and Dean's performance at its best.

To televise figure skating, to direct cameras on figure skating, requires restraint. Figure skating is artistic, it is beautiful. It requires

192

Author with Princess Anne at the Sarajevo Winter Olympics, 1984.

the clever use of two, possibly three, cameras, but most of the performance should be shot on one camera, only occasionally mixing, slowly, to another camera just to illustrate some beautiful artistic movement, such as a high-velocity spin.

Our Yugoslavian producer didn't quite see figure skating in the same way. He possibly was used to covering drag racing, or perhaps speedway. He had seven cameras at the ice stadium, and he was determined to use them all. Nothing skilful, but cut, cut, cut and cut again. Nothing gentle, like a graceful mix from one camera to another, but bang, bang, bang, bang, cut, cut, cut, all the time. I was worried when I saw his coverage of the pairs final; I was very concerned when I saw his way of thinking on the men's final; but after I saw his production efforts of Torvill and Dean's short programme, the paso doble, which brought the stadium crowd to its feet and brought forth 5.9s from all the judges, I was horrified. During that short two-minute dance there were 31 cuts!

I protested to the Yugoslavian organisers. I offered our own Jim Reside as a director – Jim was assisting Alan Weeks on all the figure skating – but they weren't interested. 'Slovovich is one of our finest directors. He covers football every week very professionally.'

193

We had our own single camera at the ice stadium, positioned alongside the dressing rooms in order to obtain interviews with the Brits competing in the various figure-skating events, knowing that this was going to be in one event only, the ice dancing, where we stood an excellent chance of winning a medal. This camera also had its own radio link back to our control room within the international broadcasting centre, and its own vision and sound line, which could, if need be, go direct, live, to London. Out came the American dollars. A few hundred, about a thousand in all, disappeared into the pockets of officials, etc., and we positioned our camera right alongside the ice rink. On that night in February 1984, the viewers at home saw Torvill and Dean come onto the ice amidst about 12 different camera cuts by our Yugoslavian director, and then, just as they paused, clasped together, waiting for the first note of Ravel's *Bolero*, just then, back in our control room I cut to the output of our single news camera. For the next four minutes we saw T & D make love on ice. It was nigh impossible to fault the British pair's interpretation of Ravel's hauntingly repetitive music, which has no change in tempo. This symbolic dance of death, so admirably original and perfectly performed, inspired the judges to award an unbroken row of nine sixes for artistic presentation. For five solid minutes the whole of the stadium was on its feet applauding the Brits. By now I had cut back to the Yugoslavian output, just on the last note of the *Bolero*. I looked around our control room and there was hardly a dry eye.

The two 'kids" efforts gave Britain a gold medal for ice skating for the third Olympics running.

For Torvill and Dean's performance alone the Winter Olympics were worth televising, especially as it was the output of a single BBC newsreel camera that captivated our audience of 24 million, and which remains for posterity on the library shelves. Within 24 hours 37 TV networks had requested copies of our one camera coverage.

By February 1984 I had made eight visits to Los Angeles. ABC of America were to be our host broadcasting network, but to give them their due they were now more than aware of their shortcomings at Lake Placid in 1980. My first visit to Los Angeles, in September 1980, was to get to know the place. It certainly is vast – 42 miles

BBC temporary control room, day before start of Games. Director Jim Reside
testing all equipment.

The control 'Gallery' at Los
Angeles, 1984.

BBC video tape area.
Los Angeles, 1984.

long by 10 miles wide. Even four years before the event I paid particular attention to the various hotels, and in the following January I went nap on one, the Wilshire Sheraton, and booked 100 of the 120 rooms with a sizeable deposit. About 10 months later the 'Organisation', as it is known in America, were given the hotel and local transport rights in connection with the 1984 Olympic Games. Between January 1981 and July 1984 a lot of pressure was put upon the hotel and me, in connection with rebooking through the Organisation, but I had an agreement with The Sheraton and they stuck by it. The Organisation ensured that during the Games, the press bus, indeed any transport facilities, did not come to our hotel. But I got what I wanted at half the price I would have had to pay the Organisation.

The Organising Committee of the LA Games, plus the Mayor's Office, was embarrassed by the pressure being put upon me by the Organisation as far as our accommodation was concerned. I was wined and dined by the Mayor's Office, and at our dinner Mayor Tom Bradley told me of a very unusual agreement they had come to with the Organisation. It was accepted by all sides concerned that amongst the many hundreds of thousands of visitors to LA the terrorists would be expected to arrive. The LA Council and the Organisation agreed that all their employers, members, crooks, etc., call them what you like, would leave the city 10 days before the Games commenced, returning two days after the Games had finished. This was so that the LA Police Department could concentrate on all the visiting bad boys, knowing that the professional crooks were out of town. When the time came, i.e. 10 days before the commencement, they all left town, a paid vacation, most of them aiming for Las Vegas. Those that were not high up the ladder, were *sponsored* by the wealthy members; they made them an offer they couldn't refuse!

There were hardly any misdemeanours. No burglaries, no car thefts, no muggings, no crime. Just a few drunks, and occasionally a bit of speeding. All of these were handled with just a warning. I was stopped twice myself for speeding. Everyone could just walk around without any worries whatsoever. About 40 terrorists were arrested and deported immediately. Six were tried and remained in the States for a very, very long time.

* * *

The Games were well run, and the enthusiasm for the events was astonishing. During the riding segment of the very first competition of the Games, the modern pentathlon, nearly 10,000 spectators turned up for what is known in the business as 'grass growing'. There were gigantic crowds for the soccer and, as expected, the track and field. And it was in these events that I very nearly released the most unbelievable news to the world.

It was the 1500 metres and we, Great Britain, had three men in the final: Seb Coe, Steve Cram and Steve Ovett. Now, both Coe and Ovett had competed in the 800 metres final four days earlier, Coe getting the silver, but Ovett struggling to finish fourth. So off went the gun for the start of the so-called 'blue riband' event of the Games, the 1500 metres. The three Brits were all up in the first five during the first two laps, then halfway around the third lap Steve Ovett dropped out, ran onto the centre field, collapsed and had to be stretchered out of the arena. Coe and Cram fought off the rest of the field, with Coe taking the gold and Cram the silver medal.

Harry Carpenter, Boxing, Los Angeles, 1984.

Ron Pickering, gymnastics, Los Angeles, 1984.

Alan Weeks commentating on the 1984 Olympics at the Olympic Pool.

Ovett was taken by ambulance to the Los Angeles Jubilee Hospital with severe respiratory problems, closely followed by our own hand-held camera. Two film teams with reporters were permanently posted at the hospital and stayed there until midnight, when I decided one team could return to the hotel whilst the other remained on duty.

At about 3 o'clock in the morning I was woken by the phone. 'Alec. Got bad news for you. Steve Ovett has passed away. He's dead.' The line also went dead. Now, I have found I always want just a few seconds to come to when woken from a deep sleep. I didn't recognise the voice. No name was given. Yet I knew perfectly, exactly what was said. I rang the other reporting team and told them to return to the hospital immediately. I rang London and relayed the information to them, finishing with 'I've yet to get this confirmed'. I quickly jumped into some clothes and dashed down to the car park. At that time in the morning the streets were clear. I was there within 15 minutes. I dashed in. There in the foyer was a pacing cameraman, behind him on benches the reporter and sound technician, both fast asleep. I glanced from one to the other. 'Nothing is happening, Alec, so we are taking it in shifts for one of us to stay awake, on duty for an hour each.' I shouted out something which woke the other two. I gabbled out my information. They looked startled and then the three dashed off in different directions, each to verify what I had told them. They had the hospital well and truly surveyed. After a couple of minutes, during which our other crew had arrived, they returned. Nothing wrong. Ovett was sleeping peacefully. 'I actually saw him for myself. The nurse reckons he will be able to return to the team camp by early morning.'

I suddenly flew for the phone and rang London. Teams of people had been collating a visual obituary that would have been ready to go on air in 10 minutes. We were that close to what would have been a broadcasting disaster of great magnitude. Just to clarify to London that Ovett was still alive, we got an interview with the athlete before he left hospital.

I later found out that our colleagues from BBC News had set this up, ringing me when they realised we had beaten them to the punch.

It's called working together!

199

Los Angeles Olympic Games opening ceremony, 1984.

David Coleman at the Los Angeles Olympic Games, 1984.

Chapter Twelve

A Winter's Tale (Tail)

On cold, frosty days, with the ice and the snow dripping from the branches, it is nice to recall those days of scurrying into Broadcasting House or Television Centre, into our centrally heated offices, studios, etc. Unhealthy, yes, but oh so lovely and warm. But if you worked in outside broadcast, one's Christmas list was headed with requests for gloves, scarves, thick socks, fur-lined jackets, and of course thermal long johns, etc. The open spaces seemed to be the coldest places on earth, and certainly football stadiums must be at the top of that list. From December onwards one seemed to be making hundreds of calls to our weather people at Television Centre, trying to work out where the frost and snow would *not* be by the weekend. In my case, with *Match of the Day*, this meant working out what matches would eventually be played on the forthcoming Saturday afternoon. It didn't matter that the temperature could be below freezing, or that the cameras would be very close to freezing up, just as long as 22 footballers would be playing a match that Saturday afternoon. Now, remember those words.

That was the situation that had been facing me one January a few years back. These were the days of hard no-quarter-given competition from ITV. They also had to find a match, or in their case five matches. We were all trying to look into the crystal ball. I elected to put all my cards into the north-west and go for Manchester City v. Wimbledon, and let ITV worry about the north-east, Midlands, London and the south. It was my opinion that Manchester City had the finest undersoil heating in the Football League: I had watched them slowly, methodically, install it at Maine Road. I knew the staff there – the manager, the secretary, the groundsman – as well as most of the players; if they wanted the

201

match to be played, the weather had to be atrocious for the game to be postponed. But it was atrocious, and getting worse. No snow, but bitter, hard frosts and dark-grey skies. As the week wore on the weather gradually took its toll and by Thursday ITV were reduced to two matches, one in the south and one in the Midlands; all my cards were on the Maine Road game.

I travelled up to Manchester on the Friday, arriving about the same time as the OB crew and equipment. 'Should we rig in?', 'Should we install *all* the equipment?' were the questions being fired at me. 'Yes,' I replied. 'No worries about this match.' I hoped I was sounding confident. My God, but it was cold. I walked on the pitch with Stan Gibson, the groundsman. It was like concrete. 'See,' he said, banging his heel into the ground and making a sound that reverberated around the empty stadium, 'with a little bit of heat that will be playable tomorrow.' A little bit of heat! There wasn't enough heat in the entire north-west of England to defrost this pitch. My spirits were getting lower and lower. Stan saw this. 'Look, I'll put the heating on nice and early, about 4 o'clock this afternoon. Not the usual seven or half-past. I've already arranged for the referee to stay away until 11.30 tomorrow.' I stopped feeling suicidal. Who knows, miracles are possible.

After attending to a few technical problems I left Maine Road for my hotel, having got Stan Gibson's promise that he would ring me in the morning, about 7.30, with his thoughts. I heard later that evening that ITV's match in the south had been cancelled. One more down, only two matches left. I felt certain that ours would be off and just wanted ITV to suffer too. With those lovely Christian thoughts in my head I slept soundly until just after six. The phone woke me. I picked it up. 'Alec, it's me, Stan.' Before I could make a rude comment, he said, 'You've got to get down here. At once.' 'What's up, what's happened?' I mumbled, and followed it with an even more stupid remark, 'Is everything OK?' 'Get down here, quickly. I'll be waiting for you by the main door,' Stan said, and he put the phone down. I was up, dressed and downstairs hailing a taxi within 5 minutes. I glanced at my watch: it was 6.15 a.m. The taxi driver looked at me twice at my request to get to the Maine Road ground 'quickly'. He did it in six minutes.

Stan was at the top of the steps when I jumped out of the cab at a run. I opened my mouth to say something as I approached Stan, but he put his finger to his lips to whisper me into silence.

He beckoned me to follow him. We moved into the club foyer, sharp left down the stairs to the dressing-room area and through to the big door leading to the players' tunnel. Once through the door, he stepped over to the large switchboard and threw down four large switches with a clang. The stadium floodlights lit up the tunnel. We moved down towards the pitch. As we got to the mouth of the tunnel, about 20 feet from the pitch, I stopped. It wasn't the white-frosted green that I had expected would greet me. It was a kaleidoscope of colour: white, black, grey, brown, ginger. A noise was reverberating around the empty stadium. A throbbing, humming sound. The flare from the floodlights made the sight seem even more macabre; the beams of light emphasised the white steam that seemed to be erupting from the pitch, or what one could see of the pitch. It was covered in cats. Feline creatures. Moggies. Dozens and dozens of them. Stan interrupted my thoughts. 'You see, Alec, I put the undersoil heating on early, as promised, just after four. Put it on full. Turned in about eleven. You got me on edge yesterday. By the early hours the pitch was quite warm and word must have gone around to all the cats in Moss Side. So I was up and shaving by five and drifted out here about half-past. If I had rung you and told you about this at 7.30 you wouldn't have believed me. I had to get you down to see it with your own eyes.'

He walked to the edge of the pitch and gently eased, with his toe, one of the 'night lodgers' away from the touchline. 'Come here. Feel the give.' I joined him and drove my heel into the pitch. This time no noise, just a faint thud, but a marvellous give of about an inch. My heart jumped. This match would be on. 'No, no,' said Stan, 'not with your foot, but with your fingers. Your hand.' I bent down and pressed my fingers into the pitch. It gave just a little. As I straightened up Stan remarked, 'Now smell your fingers.' I was still in the trancelike state that the sight I had witnessed had put me in, and I was automatically doing what Stan had requested. Wow! That brought me back. Thank God I hadn't had breakfast. We tried to count the number of Moss Side moggies and dried up at about two hundred and fifty. Word had certainly got round. You can imagine the comments in catty language. 'Hey, wacker, have you heard about the warm pad at Maine Road. Spread the word and get over there!' I stood there. Just a few feet into the pitch. Two or three of them snuggled up to my ankles looking for even more warmth. There were big cats and small cats, fat cats

203

and skinny cats, alley cats and pedigree cats, cats with scrawny torn ears, cats with beautiful fluffy round faces. The hypnotic purring was quietly all around one, and the white breath from all these hundreds of moggies rose slowly in the very, very cold air. I had never seen a sight like it. It is one I do not expect to see again in my lifetime. Stan produced a hip flask from his pocket. 'I've toasted a few things in my time, but never 250 moggies from Moss Side, Manchester, at 6.30 in the morning!'

I went back to my hotel for a celebration breakfast. As I walked into my room, where I still had to wash and shave, the phone was ringing. It was Tony Book, the City Manager. 'You've seen Stan, you've seen the pitch?' said Tony after the hellos. 'Now, Alec, promise me you won't breathe a word about this to anyone.' 'Tony, this is a great story,' I started to say. 'Listen, Alec, we've got you a match. Now you owe us. You owe me.' I agreed. I did. All I had prayed for the previous night was a match. At any cost. 'After 3.00,' Tony continued, 'after the kick-off, I don't care a damn who you tell. Until kick-off time keep your mouth closed.' That's why Tony and I always got on so well. Like me, he always spoke his mind. A wily campaigner, he certainly had something in mind, but I didn't want to know. I would keep quiet.

When I returned to the ground at about 10 a.m., Stan had eased our furry friends away. 'Put the bloody heating off. That shifted them. They were getting like Rothschilds. I'll put it back on again shortly.' The referee came and went, delighted with the condition of the pitch. 'The finest in the country,' he told the directors in the board room. 'This will be the only match on today.' The West Brom match (ITV's last-remaining fixture) was called off at 10. By now I was 10 feet tall. I couldn't grow any higher. Or could I? I didn't say a word about the 'Moggies from Manchester' to commentator Barry Davies as we rehearsed.

It was still bitterly cold, but the public turned up in their thousands to see the only football match played that day. Thanks to the undersoil heating and, yes, to groundsman Stan Gibson and 'his helpers'! Come 2.45 p.m. and we started to record the opening to that day's *Match of the Day*. A few minutes later the teams trotted out. Manchester City won the toss and kicked off. It was rather an unusual game they played, keeping the ball very low at all times, almost permanently on the ground if they could, especially in the goalmouth areas. This meant that the Wimbledon players were

'*MOTD*' technical vehicles, i.e. the OB (outside broadcast) 'scanner'.

In the '70s it took 2 men to carry a camera. Nowadays one could carry one on the little finger.

scrambling and slithering around on the ground for most of the time. Imagine the smell!

By half-time Manchester City were leading by four goals to nil. The same tactics were used for the second half, with Manchester City running out winners by five goals to one. In the interview after the match Tony Book referred to the unusual playing conditions!

The Wimbledon players very nearly missed their train back to London. They had spent an extra-long time in the bath!

By the by, I told Barry Davies over the talkback at half-time about our Manchester moggies' night on the pitch. He thought I was having him on. He didn't believe me. He does now. It's true. You ask the moggies around Moss Side, Manchester, and of course the moggies' Father Christmas, groundsman Stan Gibson.

When, today, I hear comments on television about the efforts of certain members of the staff, or club, to ensure that an event takes place, I just think of the efforts of the moggies from Manchester that cold, cold night in January past.

Chapter Thirteen

These I Have Loved

Since 1941 I have seen many changes and developments within the BBC and within all aspects of broadcasting, radio and television. Compare music alone, the era of 'the big band sound' with today's melodies. Compare the black-suited announcer with today's relaxed DJ, or, staying with sport, how would Bobby Moore have handled Wayne Rooney? Or David Beckham tackle Bobby Charlton? It is impossible to compare.

The mid-sixties technical development in broadcasting equipment alone revolutionised the operating methods of all radio and TV transmissions. More cameras and microphones were available for coverage of sport, this effect was felt within the studios with the advent of video tape. Autocue became a regular assistant to the presenter. The days of the reporter reading from a word or two scribbled on the packet of cigarettes were gone. Enter the type of presenter who would become addicted to autocue to such an extent that to remember twelve words at the start or finish of *Match of the Day* without autocue would be a tall order.

I was weaned into the broadcasting mode that the talking head was used for the purpose of linking from one event to another or, even more basic, television is all about pictures, and that the spoken word should be used for the purpose of amplifying the picture. So we therefore come to my pet hate of the modern day presentation of sport on television.

TALK, TALK, TALK, and more talk. It is said that a very senior member of the Sports Department once complained that '... the action was getting in the way of the interview...' There was a time when The Cup Final was all about presenting The Cup Final Day. Be it a transmission start at 10.30 or 12.00. Present the atmosphere, the crowds, the streets, the personalities. Not three ex-footballers sitting in a studio overlooking the pitch and forecasting, prophesying, what is going to happen in so many hours' time, and often all three experts are talking at once so that no one can hear or understand what is being said.

But it is not our presenter's fault if music is played behind practically everything. I am just waiting for the day when a football match is transmitted 'live' to the accompaniment of music. What will be played behind the goal? The *1812 Overture*!

But having said all that, the presentation of the event, the direction of the outside broadcast, is highly professional. With all the equipment they now have available, so it should be. But there are still a few commentators who do not know the difference between a radio or television commentary.

During my fifty-odd years with the BBC I have been fortunate to work with the giants in broadcasting, many of whom I have already mentioned in earlier chapters: Eamon Andrews, David Coleman, Angus McKay, Ken Wolstenholme, and Peter Dimmock; but there are others, sometimes many others. Some are broadcasting heroes, others back-room boys (or girls) but all are professionals to their fingertips and all I have worked with for many hours on many programmes. Broadcasting would be poorer without their great craftsmanship.

PETER DIMMOCK. Thousands of words have been and will be written about this man, to me the founder of BBC's outside broadcast department, who back in the '40s and early '50s, produced, directed and commentated on every event before handing it over to his contemporaries. He produced the 1953 Coronation, he introduced *Sportsview* for 10 years and *Grandstand* when it started. He 'found' every commentator of any repute back in the '50s: Peter O'Sullevan, Harry Carpenter, David Coleman, Eddie Waring. He personally insisted on interviewing and appointing every producer in the outside broadcast department. He set very, very high standards. He should have moved up to at least Director of Television, but with many,

Peter Dimmock with the author.   © BBC

many disappointments, he left us to work for American television.
He was our founder.

CLIFF MORGAN. A brilliant Welsh rugby player. A famous
broadcaster. A well respected head of the most powerful Sports
Department in the world of broadcasting. Yes, Cliff was all of
those. Twenty-nine Welsh caps and a member of the British Lions
1955 touring side of South Africa. He started broadcasting as a
freelance in 1958 and joined the BBC staff as editor of *Grandstand*
and *Sportsview* in 1964. He left to go freelance in 1966. Had a
stroke in 1972, but being Cliff, rejoined the BBC as Head of Radio
Outside Broadcasts Department, being promoted to the same position
in television in 1976. He held this job until he was asked to retire
at the age of 57 in 1987. Thank God though, he returned to radio
and to broadcasting and from 1987 to 1998 he introduced *Sport
on Four*. What was Cliff's great attribute as a man to work for?
He would listen to programme ideas, advising or correcting whenever
necessary. He would listen to complaints, moans, grouses and, above
all, treat everyone as equal. In the bar he would listen to bawdy
gossip and good old-fashioned humour and laugh side by side,

209

cheek by cheek, with the highest or the lowest in the department. A great leader. A pal; who overcame a terrible illness in 2005.

PAUL FOX. *Sportsview* and *Grandstand* were his editorial babies. He weaned them from the ideas stage. *Sportsview* made its name on the evening of 6th May 1954 with the running of the 4-minute mile by Roger Bannister, which was transmitted on *Sportsview* within an hour of it happening.

He later became Controller of BBC One, and together with David Attenborough as BBC Two's Controller, the pair worked under the Director of Television, Huw Wheldon. With these three at the helm, the BBC entered a very rich and powerful period in the world of television.

DAVID COLEMAN. If you can work with someone whose brain is lightning quick, who is reliable and brilliant, will not suffer fools easily, and whose brusqueness sometimes offends, then you'll enjoy working with David Coleman. Without doubt the finest broadcaster the world of sport will ever know.

Michael Grade, Chairman of BBC and David Coleman.

210

And he had great courage. Our first occasion of working together illustrates that. It was 1959 and I had been working in television in Manchester for a few months when I got a phone call from Paul Fox in London. '... and we want to know how far, how long, are we away from having betting shops in the High Street. Manchester seems to be the centre, the hub, of all the illegal betting and gambling saloons. So if we send up David Coleman just to meet one or two of the lads in control...' So we left it that David would come up that day and meet me at Broadcasting House, which then was positioned in Manchester Piccadilly. It so happened that the biggest, most powerful illegitimate gambling club in the North was just behind Broadcasting House. I was a member. Connections in the fight game can be useful.

We met, had a drink, then I led the way round the corner to 'The Club'. The doormen, the strong-arm-men, were expecting us and I signed David in as a visitor. Now this place was something special; a luxurious bar, an equally opulent dining room, then the gambling room with all the familiar tables for blackjack, roulette, etc, and at one end The Betting Shop. Now in 1959 the only legal betting that could take place was 'on course' betting at the race courses and dog tracks. There had been racing at Manchester that afternoon so the Club was busy.

I forgot to mention: anyone who had a position of importance in the Manchester 'underworld' was a member of the club. This worried me more than anything else. How would these particular members react to David's inquisitive questioning? By then, of course, he had been appearing on *Grandstand* regularly and was a welcome friend in everyone's lounge. They, the members, greeted him like an old friend, answering all his questions. This went on for some time until we found ourselves in the middle of a group of very powerful men – powerful in the Manchester 'underworld'. They included four of the most ruthless, notorious criminals in the North. Broad-shouldered, thick-necked, the odd broken nose, or twisted ear. But, between them they controlled gambling in Manchester. Within a few seconds of my introducing David they relaxed, smiling, and treated him like an old friend. By eleven he had answers to all his questions. A real professional investigative journalist. Courageous. I learnt a lot about him that evening.

It took me some months and hundreds of hours of broadcasting to understand him. But when I eventually did, I appreciated his brilliance. Born in 1926, he worked on local northern newspapers before joining the BBC in Birmingham in 1954. He worked on all the regional news programmes, sport, radio and television, and for three years learnt his trade. Then in 1957 he was brought to London Lime Grove Studios to introduce a programme that had just started – *Grandstand*.

That year, 1957, saw the rise of two names in the world of sport as *Grandstand* and David Coleman grew in stature together. Being a former international miler, he took to athletics commentary like a duck to water, and up to the turn of the century was still one of the finest athletics commentators. We broadcast together all the White City athletics from '65 to '68. Soccer was another sport he covered. In my opinion, in the '70s on soccer and athletics, he could not be bettered in the world.

His greatest attribute as a commentator was to say what the man on the street was thinking as the ball thundered towards the goal. He is the cloth-cap supporter standing on the terrace. He set himself very, very high standards. He expected everyone else to do so, otherwise he could be awkward, ranting and raving at someone or other. But, when the chips were really down, when technical breakdowns of cameras, monitors, or at times, both, meant nothing but disaster, he would perform as if nothing had happened and, at all times, ensure the viewers missed nothing. He would be a tower of strength. Incidentally, when things like that happened, the noise and shouting within the scanner, the mobile control room, would be deafening, chaotic, to say the least. David would hear all this and just carry on speaking in a very calm, cool manner.

I enjoyed doing the 'big ones' with him. Wembley Stadium. Cup Final day. About quarter past two, 25 minutes before the teams came on to the pitch, Des Lynam or Frank Bough would hand over to the commentator, David Coleman. David would say over his special talkback, 'OK, big man, I'll follow your pictures,' and for a solid 45 minutes before kick-off we all relaxed and got the shots that reflected the enjoyment of the day, and by the time the kick-off came all tension and nerves had disappeared. It was like that in 1976 when BAFTA decided our Cup Final coverage earned the award of 'The Best Outside Broadcast Coverage of the Year'. We worked together from 1959 until 1990.

Unfortunately I have always been aware that we have robbed

Author with *BAFTA* Award, 1976.
© *Coventry Evening Telegraph*

the medical world by forcing David to concentrate on broadcasting. If you are feeling 'off colour', he knows exactly what treatment you require. If one's ailment is physical David Coleman is the person who knows the perfect treatment. I recall the occasion when I lay in the recovery room coming round from an operation on my knee. The phone rang alongside me. A beautiful nurse answered it, listened, then quietly handed the phone to me. It was David at the other end, wanting to know how I had got on and, in detail, what had been done. I really was in agony but managed to give him all the gory details. 'Who did this? What's his name ... ?' I told him. 'Well,' he shouted, 'it's all wrong. It will take you months to recover and you'll most probably walk with a limp for the rest of your life.' He then slammed down the phone. I felt bad before he rang. Now I felt suicidal. The medical world just do not know what they are missing.

BRYAN COWGILL. From 1957, he was Sports Department's first Executive Producer, in charge of *Sportsview* and *Grandstand*, working alongside editor Paul Fox. Bryan became TV's first Head of Sport in 1962 and in 1973 he became Controller of BBC One. He expected perfection from all of his staff. God help you if he didn't get it. Without a doubt a brilliant Producer of Sport. He left the BBC in 1978 to become Programme Controller of ITV.

There were many commentators I enjoyed working with. To name a few:

HARRY CARPENTER. The most underrated broadcaster from the mid-sixties until his retirement in the middle nineties. His first TV boxing commentary was in 1949 and, having seen practically every Heavyweight Championship since 1955, it was for this sport he became justly famous and, in the eyes of the public, the most respected. But he also introduced programmes such as *Grandstand*, *Sportsnight*, major Golf Championships, Wimbledon, and commentated on dozens and dozens of other sporting events. Harry would have a go at any sport, providing he had enough time to 'do his homework', do his preparation, because it was here that his great asset existed. Spending hours, sometimes days, beforehand on research. As far as I am concerned his greatest ability was his attitude to television. His humility. He knew his job was only as important as the cameraman's or lighting engineer's, no more, no less. He never put himself above the crew, always mixing with them, eating with them. Harry Carpenter knows that television is very much a team effort and that he was just one of the cogs in the wheel.

PETER ALLISS. I was amazed to learn Peter has been commentating since 1965, having followed and learnt so much about the art from the great Henry Longhurst. His warm, clear voice relays the intricate art of golf; of the strokes, the skill, even the thoughts within the player's brain.

PETER O'SULLEVAN. I never produced Peter. That was impossible. I often directed the races he commented on. Took me some time to get used to his habit of appearing about a couple of minutes before '...cue Peter'. Always calm for three quarters of the race but then building into the fastest, clearest commentary of the racing calendar.

BILL McLAREN. Another example of making a complicated game clear and understandable to the viewer, but in a warm Scottish brogue. Without doubt the finest rugby commentator of our time.

214

KEN WOLSTENHOLME. As mentioned earlier, Ken was also a pathfinder in televised soccer, with a good memory for player identification and of incidents – bookings, penalties, etc. The slow-motion replay machines came into soccer TV a few years before Ken left us.

Barry Davies commentating at Wembley.

BARRY DAVIES. Joined us in 1969 and took a few years to 'settle in', but by '71 was doing four of five matches a month. It was my opinion that, as soon as he started covering tennis, badminton, athletics, gymnastics and ice skating, as well as his beloved soccer, he moved into 'the upper class' of international commentators.

RON PICKERING. Big Ron. Big in every way. He may not have had the speedy technique of Coleman, but his knowledge of athletics, especially field events, made him famous throughout the world. What a likeable fellow he was with his beautiful sense of humour. He passed away at the peak of his career.

Eddie Waring

EDDIE WARING. A great northerner, who put rugby league on the map. His lovely dry sense of humour and natural northern way of speaking his mind made him loved by everyone. His '...ups and unders' and his '...he's for an early bath' will be remembered by all.

ALAN WEEKS. Prior to his death in 1996 we had been receiving each other's mail for years and years. We are not related, we just worked for the same firm. Born in 1924, he made his name in ice hockey, and though he became famous for his ice skating commentary, during his 25 years with the BBC he commentated on 25 different sports. There is not a commentator, in British television today, who could do that. He was good. Very, very good. His name was Weeks.

Before I leave the TV presenters and commentators, let me say that it seemed a very black day when Jimmy Hill and Des Lynam left 'the Beeb' for ITV. It was the end of Sports Department as far as the written press were concerned and even for the pessimists within the department. They had obviously completely overlooked the youngsters 'standing in the wings': Gary Lineker, Sue Barker, Hazel Irving, Clare Balding, Steve Cram and Michael Johnson, who slid into the major programmes like true experienced professionals. Together with the vastly experienced John Inverdale, the commercial networks have got a lot to worry about.

Some producers and directors also became world-famous through the skills they perfected whilst working on the BBC's outside broadcasts:

ANTHONY CRAXTON. Some may recall the name. Producer of many ceremonial events, the mammoth outside broadcasts of Princess Anne's wedding, Winston Churchill's funeral, etc., i.e. those involving 30 to 40 cameras (which was normal). On transmission he was helpful and knowledgeable, calmly telling one cameraman what to expect and what type of shot to offer as the procession came into view. After I had carried out a mammoth OB, such as the Cup Final, he would always have a word of encouragement or praise.

ALAN CHIVERS. Another 'Great' from the '60s. A member of Fighter Command, he joined the BBC in 1946. His greatest production was *The Old Man of Hoy*. He was executive producer of the '66 World Cup for all external broadcasts. During his final ten years Alan was in charge of all the major overseas sporting events. In his mid-80s he still looked like a young 60-year-old. Couldn't have been a bad life after all.

ALAN MOUNCER. A great director. He improved on every sport he covered, using different techniques and camera positions. He covered every sport, though he specialised in athletics and gymnastics, making the world sit up with his production techniques. He left the BBC in the mid-70s.

JIM RESIDE. Worked on *Match of the Day* as a cameraman, a stage manager, production assistant and finally a producer, where he directed hundreds of matches. A unique record. In his spare time he produced the ice-skating shows, gymnastics and the Winter Olympics from '88 to 2002. Chuck in the 1990 Italian World Cup and one questions the sanity that prevailed to give this experienced individual early retirement in his early 50s.

217

JOHN SHREWSBURY. His calm, imaginative productions were his showcase. He specialised in golf, athletics and soccer, and was executive producer for soccer from 1984 to 1999.

MARTIN HOPKINS was one of the few producers who would not accept early retirement and carried on producing *Grandstand*, *Sports Personality of the Year* and all the Summer Olympics from 1988 through to 2004, working through the historic John Birt period. In 2003 he was awarded the OBE. He earned it.

DEWI GRIFFITHS. Cardiff-based, he set the standard in the '70s and '80s for all Rugby Union productions.

JOHN McGONIGLE. Based at Birmingham, John directed soccer and cricket from 1964 until 1981, including all the Middlesbrough '66 World Cup matches. He was a member of the BBC team at Mexico in 1970 and Germany in 1974.

RAY LAKELAND. working out of Manchester, he was one of the great unheralded producers of TV sport. For 20 years he blazed a trail in the north, including the production of the first televised Aintree Grand National in 1960. In 1966 he directed all the Sheffield World Cup matches.

One always has to have a strong production team. One relies on them. Call them 'leg-men', 'caption assistants', 'stage managers', they carried out a mountain of jobs and were often responsible for doing the impossible. Operators like JIMMY DUMINGHAN, ROY NORTON, BILL PLATTS; thank God they were on my side.

The engineers. One could name hundreds, but those who will always stand out in my memory as being the very tops in their job were:

NORMAN TAYLOR, who accompanied me on many an overseas trip and really showed the world what BBC technical engineering was all about.

TED BRAGG, who sat alongside me on so many occasions, but in particular during the 1966 World Cup, and gave me so much brilliant support.

ALAN ROBERTS, who was my engineering manager on so many Cup Finals, sweated blood for me when the 'technical hitches' appeared, but who made it all appear perfect on the screen.

CLIVE POTTER. Tall, well-built, bow-tie, etc. A damn good engineer to work with, in the last ten years showing the youngsters how to light TV shows.

ANGUS McKAY. The founder of radio sport in the late 1940s. He built the foundation on which today's excellent radio sport programmes are presented on Radio Five Live. The technical improvements of outside broadcasts have enabled radio to invade corners which even television cannot reach. Angus set that pattern.

DAVE GORDON. A follower in the footsteps of Paul Fox. Worked well with producer Martin Hopkins on the major events. He is well-respected in the world of televised sport.

TREVOR WIMLETT. One of the world's best television cameramen. A good diplomat, as well as being a brilliant interpreter of the director's wishes. Some directors are such cowards they do nothing but take all the credit for the great shots afterwards. It is the Trevor Wimletts of this world who interpret the action as it happens. To him, everything is live, is happening now. He's come to me after three hours' non-stop on a camera, his eyes bloodshot, the imprint of the viewfinder still hard on his face, his forehead streaked with drying sweat. 'Everything OK? Were you happy?' If not, he was prepared to spend another three hours listening to advice on how

The low camera in a three-foot pit at Wembley.

to improve the coverage. There were many cameramen of a similar ilk, such as: PHIL WILSON, TEDDY COCKS, SELWYN COX, BARRY CHASTON and TONY WIGLEY.

Pat Ewing (now Mrs Cliff Morgan) outside BBC Radio's Los Angeles mobile control studio.

PAT EWING. The first woman to occupy the position of Head of Sport and Outside Broadcast *Radio*. She had the natural ability to lead and allow operators to do their job. She later started and ran Radio Five. She was the one who started it all, but never received her due credit from the Beeb.

THE PRODUCER'S ASSISTANT. Three stand out as far as I'm concerned. These are the people who really are the producer's left and right hands, the memory bank, the computer brain, the adviser, besides being the secretary, the typist, the computer operator, etc., etc. Often, after disasters, they also had to dry the producer's eyes, pat them on the head and send them out again. All with the ability to work tirelessly and loyally alongside you. In my mind the three are: ANN FOSTER, LESLEY MORRIS and PENNY WOOD.

These have, in their own way, left their mark on the world of broadcasting; commentators, producers, the engineers, all the 'boys and girls'. They have all allowed me to work alongside them. These are the backbone and the true spirit of the BBC and it is to them and to 'Auntie' I say, 'Thank you for having me'.

Chapter Fourteen

The Last Tweak of Auntie's Skirts

And so, relentlessly, 2nd February 1987 approached, the day I reached the age of 60 and the BBC retired me. Now, I had always trained myself to keep my feet firmly on the ground, but there were some attitudes which left me reeling. They didn't retire me earlier and give me two years' salary as compensation, which was the 'misfortune' of many of my remaining colleagues. Never mind, there was the opportunity to have a nice library of the many Cup Finals I had produced, the video cassettes of which were now commercially on sale in the various video shops; but the BBC's enterprise department, their sales department, were full of phrases like 'We do not have a budget for complimentary copies', and 'This period of austerity', or 'If you let us know where you live we will send you a list of the video shops in your area'! After I retired, I visited my local Virgin shop and paid my £9.99 for each of the video cassettes I wanted!

A few months earlier I had decided I would write my autobiography and wrote to a Chris Weller, Head of BBC Books. His reply: 'I have no doubt that many of your former colleagues would find a book by you entertaining; we are not, nevertheless, in the business of publishing the BBC for the BBC!'

During 46 years one accumulates a lot of paper, newspaper cuttings, annual books, technical manuals, recordings, tapes, films, etc. Most of my spare time during that last month was taken up with sorting out all the bric-a-brac. The TV set in the corner of the office reminded me that I had to contact someone regarding the rented set the BBC had installed at home. There were parties, lots of them, then on the Saturday my last soccer match for the Beeb, the third-round FA Cup match between Wimbledon and

Everton. I retired on the Tuesday and that evening, on the, 6th floor of Television Centre, the Director of BBC Television, Bill Cotton, gave a dinner for myself and Pamela and 30 invited guests. There was Reg Harris, Bobby Charlton, Bobby Moore, Bob Paisley, David Coleman, Cliff Morgan, etc. So from 7 o'clock until long after midnight Pamela and I were treated like royalty. Then, after many, many goodbyes a chauffeured limousine to take us all the way home to Rottingdean. And two very tired, but very happy and contented pensioners finally flopped into bed just after 3 a.m.

The ringing of the doorbell. Then the banging on the door brought forth the shattering news, 'There is someone at the door.' I was being dragged along the path of sanity and thought that either there was someone at the door or someone had decided to demolish the house. 'Your turn,' said the muffled voice alongside me. Trying to pull my thoughts together, I decided that it would be tactful, to get my retirement off to a good start, not to use my favourite phrase as in the past, 'This is the only day I get off this month.' I looked at my watch: half past eight. It felt like the middle of the night. I stumbled out of bed and downstairs, pulling on my dressing gown at the same time.

The ringing of the doorbell was now non-stop. I opened the door. Two fellows were standing there, dressed in overalls with the name of a Spanish town on the breast-pocket – Granada. The older one stepped forward.

'We've come to collect your television set,' said the spokesman.

I realised then that my BBC days were over. Auntie had swished her skirts, turned on her heels and closed the door.

Index

228

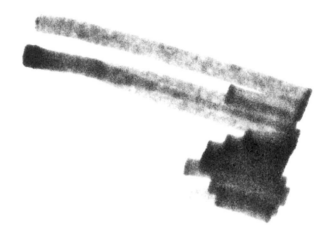